YORK NOTES

The Scarlet Letter

Nathaniel Hawthorne

Notes by Julian Cowley

 Longman   York Press

The right of Julian Cowley to be identified as Author of this Work has been asserted by him in accordance with the Copyright, Designs and Patents Act 1988

YORK PRESS
322 Old Brompton Road, London SW5 9JH

PEARSON EDUCATION LIMITED
Edinburgh Gate, Harlow,
Essex CM20 2JE, United Kingdom
Associated companies, branches and representatives throughout the world

© Librairie du Liban *Publishers* and Addison Wesley Longman Limited 1999

First published 1999
Second impression 2000

ISBN 0-582-41473-3

Designed by Vicki Pacey, Trojan Horse, London
Phototypeset by Gem Graphics, Trenance, Mawgan Porth, Cornwall
Colour reproduction and film output by Spectrum Colour
Produced by Pearson Education China Limited, Hong Kong

C ONTENTS

PART ONE

INTRODUCTION

HOW TO STUDY A NOVEL

Studying a novel on your own requires self-discipline and a carefully thought-out work plan in order to be effective.

- You will need to read the novel more than once. Start by reading it quickly for pleasure, then read it slowly and thoroughly.
- On your second reading make detailed notes on the plot, characters and themes of the novel. Further readings will generate new ideas and help you to memorise the details of the story.
- Some of the characters will develop as the plot unfolds. How do your responses towards them change during the course of the novel?
- Think about how the novel is narrated. From whose point of view are events described?
- A novel may or may not present events chronologically: the time-scheme may be a key to its structure and organisation.
- What part do the settings play in the novel?
- Are words, images or incidents repeated so as to give the work a pattern? Do such patterns help you to understand the novel's themes?
- Identify what styles of language are used in the novel.
- What is the effect of the novel's ending? Is the action completed and closed, or left incomplete and open?
- Does the novel present a moral and just world?
- Cite exact sources for all quotations, whether from the text itself or from critical commentaries. Wherever possible find your own examples from the novel to back up your opinions.
- Always express your ideas in your own words.

This York Note offers an introduction to *The Scarlet Letter* and cannot substitute for close reading of the text and the study of secondary sources.

The Scarlet Letter is a tale of illicit passion. Or rather, it is a tale of the aftermath of illicit passion, for Hester Prynne has given birth to her child before the story commences, and her love has been driven underground by the stern gaze of New England Puritanism.

Nathaniel Hawthorne writes about the fate of a sensual woman who has broken the law of a male-dominated community, and is forced to live as an outcast. The action of the tale is largely concerned with the efforts of Hester's husband, Roger Chillingworth, to discover the identity of his wife's lover. The magistrates of Boston are also engaged in this investigation, little suspecting that it is Arthur Dimmesdale, a highly respected minister, who is the culprit.

In a sense, *The Scarlet Letter* anticipates more recent detective fiction, with its clandestine meetings, clues being read, and a suspect being watched. As with that genre, we are involved as readers in what is essentially a drama of interpretation.

Nathaniel Hawthorne's work seems modern also in its concern with language. The title directs our attention to the scarlet letter 'A', attached to the breast of Hester's gown as a token of her crime. But what does that letter really signify? Increasingly we recognise that 'adulteress', the intended signification, by no means exhausts the letter's capacity to generate meaning.

Hester's daughter, Pearl, is presented as an incarnation of the scarlet letter; she is a living token of her parents' transgression. As we might expect, she is a wild child, apparently lawless. Yet she demonstrates a disarming, intuitive moral sense. How should we read this engaging little girl, who is branded as the product of sin? How does her vibrant energy stand in relation to the sombre gravity of the Puritan dignitaries? Is it to be considered a more affirmative, or more destructive quality?

We are required to make moral discriminations amongst the adult characters also, weighing the motivations for their actions against the consequences. *The Scarlet Letter* enacts a vivid psychological drama in which the desires of the individual and the regulations of society are set in conflict.

In the introductory chapter, entitled 'The Custom-House', Nathaniel Hawthorne offers a concise definition of the literary mode he has chosen for this book. He identifies it as a **romance**, and explains that this form offers just the amalgam of the Actual and the Imaginary which he requires to explore how reason and emotion blend to form human understanding. In the process it allows him to introduce some memorable **Gothic** touches.

In addition to looking forward to modern concerns and techniques, *The Scarlet Letter* also looks back. Not only is the tale set two hundred years before its date of composition, but Nathaniel Hawthorne plays skilful variations on the archaic literary mode called **allegory**. He counterpoints the limitations of that mode against the broadened horizons of modern readers, accustomed to the increasing subtleties of nineteenth-century prose fiction.

The technical boldness of the book serves to enrich our awareness of the important issues Nathaniel Hawthorne raises, concerning the nature of historical change, the value of American democracy, the rights of women and the social status of art.

PART TWO

SUMMARIES & COMMENTARIES

The first edition of *The Scarlet Letter* was limited to 2500 copies. It was published on 16 March 1850. A second edition followed in April. The Penguin Classics edition follows the authoritative text produced in 1962 by the Ohio State University Press, for the Ohio State University Center for Textual Studies. It formed Volume I of the *Centenary Edition of the Works of Nathaniel Hawthorne*, and collated the author's own manuscript with the most reliable subsequent editions. Page references conform to this edition.

SYNOPSIS

In the introductory chapter the author narrates an account of his experiences as a Surveyor in the Custom-House, in Salem, Massachusetts. There he discovered an old manuscript and a piece of faded scarlet fabric, in the form of the letter 'A'. He proceeds to tell the story which he has developed from this documentary material.

The tale is set in Boston during the 1640s. A woman named Hester Prynne is put on show in the market-place as part of her punishment for an act of adultery. In her arms she carries a baby girl, and on the breast of her gown she wears the scarlet letter 'A'. The magistrates of the town ask her to disclose the identity of the child's father. She steadfastly refuses.

From her position on the public platform, Hester recognises with horror a strange man in the crowd. It is her husband, a scholar and physician, who has assumed the name, Roger Chillingworth. On her return to prison, Hester is attended by this physician, who declares his intention to discover the name of her lover. He makes Hester promise not to reveal his own identity, as her husband.

The woman is released from prison, and lives as an outcast on the margins of the community. She undertakes needlecraft to support herself and her daughter, Pearl, but demonstrates an artistry in her work which exceeds merely functional requirements.

As Pearl grows she behaves with alarming wildness, and the authorities consider taking her from her mother. However, Hester persuades the magistrates to allow her to oversee her daughter's development.

Chillingworth takes up residence in the same lodgings as Arthur Dimmesdale, a highly respected young minister. Dimmesdale has recently shown symptoms of rapidly declining health, and the physician undertakes to monitor his wellbeing. Very soon, this constant observation assumes a profoundly sinister aspect.

The minister's discomfort is compounded by the fact that little Pearl shows a pronounced interest in him, as if she has recognised intuitively that this man is her father. Dimmesdale undergoes private agonies, racked by the anguish of concealment, as he lives his double life.

One night, under cover of darkness, he ascends the platform where Hester had endured exposure to the public gaze. By chance, she and Pearl encounter him there. An unearthly light, with the form of a scarlet 'A', appears in the sky.

Hester resolves that she must break her vow and disclose Chillingworth's identity, in order to free Dimmesdale from the physician's devilish attentions. She meets the minister in the forest, and tells him that the man who claimed to assist him is actually married to her. He is appalled at the discovery.

Hester proposes that they should escape, with Pearl, to Europe. After initial resistance, the minister eventually agrees to the plan. Hester removes the scarlet letter, but when Pearl returns from playing she insists that her mother should continue to wear the stigma.

Filled with agitated excitement at the prospect of a new life, Dimmesdale delivers the prestigious Election Sermon. At the end of it he summons Hester and Pearl to the platform and makes a public declaration of his guilt. He reveals a scarlet letter 'A' which he has etched in his own flesh, and then he dies.

Chillingworth, deprived of his prey, dies soon afterwards. Hester and Pearl disappear from Boston, but at length Hester returns to her cottage by the sea. She receives regular letters and gifts, apparently from Pearl, who is living as a wealthy lady in Europe.

On her death, Hester is buried beside Dimmesdale. Their gravestone bears a scarlet letter 'A' on a black background.

'THE CUSTOM-HOUSE' – INTRODUCTORY TO 'THE SCARLET LETTER'

The author establishes himself as narrator of this book by adopting a first-person voice in this introduction, and by relating experiences drawn from his own life, while acting as Surveyor in the Custom-House, in Salem, Massachusetts.

After describing the dilapidated building, Nathaniel Hawthorne discusses his New England ancestors. The first 'was a soldier, legislator, judge', 'a ruler in the Church', and had 'all the Puritanic traits, both good and evil' (p. 12).

He proceeds to describe his role as Surveyor, and his own aged colleagues: the Inspector and the Collector. Throughout his description he presents thinly veiled suggestions that this government institution is peculiarly prone to corrupt practice.

During this break in his literary career, Nathaniel Hawthorne discovered, he tells us, a bundle of documents left by a previous Surveyor with a penchant for antiquarian research. The most immediately intriguing part of the package is a faded piece of fine red cloth, with traces of embroidery.

Accompanying the cloth is a fairly full account of its history, and of the story of Hester Prynne. The written account of this singular woman was composed largely from oral testimony, gathered from aged members of the local community. She is remembered as a dignified and sober figure, who in later life acted as a voluntary nurse and counsellor, assisting the needy of Massachusetts.

The author now assumes the guise of editor to these materials. He comments on the thought he gave to developing the skeletal story. In the course of describing his difficulties, Nathaniel Hawthorne formulates a definition of 'romance'. He then shifts attention to the effects on his creativity of working as a civil servant.

In his 'Preface' to the book's second edition, Nathaniel Hawthorne remarked that 'The Custom-House', his 'sketch of official life' caused controversy when *The Scarlet Letter* first appeared. Some readers took its portrayal of officials as a personal attack. He suggests, with **irony**, that the book could have been issued without the offending section, but in fact 'The Custom-House' is an integral part of Nathaniel Hawthorne's artistic design in *The Scarlet Letter*. This introductory sketch establishes a number of important themes in the book, and provides clues as to how what follows should be read.

Nathaniel Hawthorne identifies himself as the narrating voice, indicating that in writing this long introductory chapter, he has been driven by an 'autobiographical impulse' (p. 7). Note that 'impulse', signifying irrational motivation, becomes a key word in the tale which follows (see Language and Style). The word may be seen to link Hester Prynne to this narrator, and it suggests the shared weaknesses and susceptibilities of all human beings.

By immediately invoking his own life, Nathaniel Hawthorne forms a bridge between the mid-nineteenth-century present, and the mid-seventeenth-century New England past, which forms the setting for the tale of 'The Scarlet Letter'. That historical dimension is important to Nathaniel Hawthorne's conception of morality. He believed that human beings had to acknowledge the past, and act responsibly towards its legacy. He also believed that we have the capacity to learn from history and to make practical improvements in the way society is organised. He saw American democracy as an important stage in that gradual amelioration.

Note that Nathaniel Hawthorne's autobiographical approach would have been familiar to his readers. It has been characteristic of much American literature that it speaks insistently from personal experience, rather than from second-hand knowledge or abstract theorising. From the start we are invited to elide the author and his narrating voice; it is prudent to exercise caution in making this identification. Nathaniel Hawthorne is assuming a distinct **persona** in order to appear in the book; that involves sustained stylisation that turns him into a semi-fictional character (see Characterisation).

It was a convention of the early-seventeenth-century English novel for authors to announce that they were acting as editors of documents that had come into their possession. A famous example of this practice is Daniel Defoe's *Robinson Crusoe* (1709). Nathaniel Hawthorne uses his introductory chapter to explain how he came into possession of the manuscript which outlines the story of the scarlet 'A'. He refers to the general example of these earlier novelistic instances, in a way that places him in **ironic** relation to that tradition. It is thematically appropriate that such a link with the European past is established.

It is also important that the narrator does not lay claim to privileged understanding of the materials. He has found them, and is relating them to us. He may suggest certain ways to read them, but he does not have the authority of an originator, or God-like figure, and that should encourage us to feel that our own acts of interpretation are equally legitimate. *The Scarlet Letter* emphasises that reading and interpreting are processes in which all human beings are necessarily engaged at all times. In this insistence, Nathaniel Hawthorne may be seen to anticipate the critical practice of semiotics (see Critical History: Contemporary Approaches).

The narrator imagines his reader to be in a relaxed conversational relationship with him. The frank informality of his tone contrasts starkly with the stern reserve of the Puritan community, described in the tale that follows. Nonetheless, he is aware as a writer of the need to protect and preserve 'the inmost Me' (p. 7). That awareness prepares us for the devilish violation of an inner self performed on Arthur Dimmesdale by Roger Chillingworth.

Salem, in Massachusetts, is the narrator's home town. In 1692, it acquired notoriety as the scene of virulent persecution of witches. One of the presiding judges was William's son, John Hathorne. (William Hathorne, 1607–81, was Nathaniel Hawthorne's great-great-great grandfather.) In the twentieth century, that persecution has been dramatised by the American playwright, Arthur Miller, in *The Crucible* (1953). It was a symptom not only of irrational religious fervour, but also of appalling intolerance towards women within a gravely patriarchal society. The eccentric Mistress

Hibbins, who appears at intervals throughout *The Scarlet Letter*, was eventually executed as a witch.

Note how Nathaniel Hawthorne makes fifty years seem like a lengthy historical span. The obvious contrast is with the Old World of Europe, steeped in tradition and burdened by the weight of history. The relative newness of American social life is played against a sense of rapid change and decay in the appearance of Salem. We are made aware of the irrevocability of passing time.

America prided itself on being a young society, but Nathaniel Hawthorne felt that after its wild childhood, time had come for the nation to recognise the responsibilities of its maturity. Just as Pearl, in the story that follows, must learn the ways of adult life and so become socialised, Nathaniel Hawthorne felt that America should pass beyond the energetic lawlessness espoused by some of his contemporaries, such as Ralph Waldo Emerson and Margaret Fuller (see Literary Background).

The eagle above the Custom-House is a national emblem, a unifying focus for the many disparate strands comprising this vast country. It is a sign to be read, and like the scarlet 'A', it is open to diverse and contrary interpretation. The 'intermingled thunderbolts and barbed arrows' (p. 9) suggest warlike predatoriness more in keeping with the empires of the Old World than the peaceful republic envisaged by Thomas Jefferson and the other founders of modern America. During the 1840s, America waged aggressive war against Mexico, the nation adjoining its south-west.

The ideals of America's Founding Fathers, those signatories in 1776 to the Declaration of Independence (see Historical Background), seem generally remote from the materialistic preoccupations of this institution for commercial regulation. Emerson and his Transcendentalist followers, who are referred to directly later in the chapter, sought to promote an idealistic philosophy in this obsessively commercial society (see Literary Background). But the energy which was crucial to Emerson's visionary America is notably lacking from the dilapidated inhabitants of the government building that Nathaniel Hawthorne describes.

The reference to 'womankind, with her tools of magic' (p. 11) conforms to the stereotypical nineteenth-century image of the home as the proper place for decent women, but it also harks back to that witch-hunting past of Salem, and helps to prepare us for the superstitious treatment which Hester Prynne receives. Hester espouses a number of beliefs which may be classed as feminist, and her rebelliousness against the patriarchal order was just the kind of symptom which would have marked her out for persecution. Nathaniel Hawthorne's own views were more moderate, and his emphasis falls persistently upon the need to find a middle course between extreme positions.

Nathaniel Hawthorne refers to his ancestors, who have inhabited the same spot for two hundred years. This is scarcely a long time in European terms, but he is concerned to stress that the New World, like the Old, exists in historical time. As a political entity modern America had only been in existence since 1776, but it did have a past that was lengthening daily, and that could not be ignored, despite Emerson's rhetorical insistence that he had no past at his back.

He uses the phrase 'the mere sensuous sympathy of dust for dust' (p. 12) to explain his sense of rootedness. The image of dust has inevitable associations of mortality, and he returns to it on the final page of the book. The word 'sympathy' is an important one for Nathaniel Hawthorne, indicating not just fellow-feeling, but the common fate of mortal human beings which should unite us all in moral understanding and compassion.

He talks of roots, and comments that 'frequent transplantation is perhaps better for the stock' (p. 12). The suggestion is that a change of environment can enable us to perceive things in a new light. Analogies between human beings and plants feature regularly in what follows. The image of America as a garden, even as the Garden of Eden, was commonplace throughout the nineteenth century, although it was used with increasing **irony** as the impact of industrialisation in the New World became increasingly apparent. Nathaniel Hawthorne may be thinking specifically of the famous image of Americans as plants relocated in new soil, in J. Hector St John de Crèvecoeur's *Letters from an American Farmer* (1782). Note his remark soon afterwards that, 'Neither the front nor the back entrance of the Custom-House opens on the road to Paradise' (p. 16).

William Hathorne's [*sic*] severe persecution of Quaker women is actually on record, but more generally this first New England ancestor of the author **personifies** a structure of social power, which is fundamentally oriented towards men and conventionally masculine values. As such he is an incarnation of that society which stigmatises and seeks to ostracise Hester Prynne. It persists in milder form in the 'patriarchal body of veterans' at the Custom-House (p. 15).

Nathaniel Hawthorne suggests that telling this tale is part of his expiation for the sins of his forefathers. He is not willing to ignore this unpalatable aspect of his family's past. He archly suggests that their guilt has met with sufficient retribution in his own person; they would not have approved of his being a writer.

Art and artistry assume major thematic importance in *The Scarlet Letter*. Nathaniel Hawthorne believed that art has the capacity to mediate between head and heart, between discipline and imagination. It may thus give a clearer and fairer sense of how human beings live than cold rational detachment or impassioned emotional response. It is Hester Prynne's artistic skills which preserve her humanity amidst adversity, and provide a means for her to gain respect from the community. Nathaniel Hawthorne is surely also indulging in self-justification in an American cultural climate that was predominantly practical and had little time for, or tradition of aesthetic pleasure. In his temporary stay at the Custom-House, he tells us, he lived remote from literature, in the company of men who cared little for the written word.

His function as Surveyor is defined as 'paternal and protective' (p. 17). His assumption of that role with regard to the old men who run the Custom-House is particularly ironic in light of Arthur Dimmesdale's abdication of paternal responsibility. Nathaniel Hawthorne recognised that the old men held their office precariously, and might readily have been sacrificed to the imperatives of efficiency; he 'could never quite find in my heart to act upon the knowledge' (pp. 16–17). His compassion enabled them to continue inefficiently in their posts. This signals clearly an authorial orientation opposing the heartless rigour of the New England Puritans. It is important to our interpretation that we recognise where his sympathies lie in such a case.

The octogenarian Inspector is characterised as having developed his 'animal nature' to 'rare perfection'. He has little evident intellect, and a 'very trifling admixture of moral and spiritual ingredients' (p. 19). He is largely governed by his appetites, and his unreflecting nature grants him a sunny, if lamentably shallow, disposition. He has survived three wives, and numerous of his twenty children have also died, but he has known little real grief.

Nathaniel Hawthorne is suggesting that this man, who is apparently blessed in his animal-like lack of self-consciousness, is actually radically deficient in his failure to connect with the moral requirements of other human beings. The humorous tone adopted here contrasts boldly with the grave study of Puritan New England which is to follow. But, later in the book, we will be told that Pearl similarly needs to experience genuine sorrow before she can enter true fellowship with human society. To support that later parallel, the narrator here discusses the similarities in outlook found in children and in the very old. They may seem happier than adults in their prime, but in both cases there is lack of a much-needed spiritual dimension.

His next sketch presents the Collector, an old soldier whose military career recalls the fierce emblematic eagle, and casts a long shadow over the ideal vision of America as a peaceful nation. Nathaniel Hawthorne presents war as another token of our Fallen condition. Like the Inspector's appetite for food, the Collector's aptitude for war highlights animalistic aspects of his nature, albeit perceived as glorious acts by the historians of warfare.

His martial spirit is described as 'a deep, red glow, as of iron in a furnace' (p. 23). The terms of this description are replicated numerous times in the subsequent discussion of the old iron-visaged Boston patriarchy and of the scarlet letter's red glow. In fact, his military demeanour is tempered by a general kindliness in his customary approach to life. This seems to suggest that he is flexible, and could amend his responses according to the occasion, in a way the Puritan leaders could not.

Conventional attributes of masculinity find expression in his character, but they are curiously coupled with a conventionally feminine appreciation of flowers. Nathaniel Hawthorne concurred with Margaret Fuller in perceiving this range of attributes to be present in all human beings. Rigid distinction of male and female characteristics is never adequate to the complex amalgam of qualities which forms an individual man or woman. Nathaniel Hawthorne clearly felt that qualities of compassion and sympathetic understanding, which had become conventionally viewed as feminine, needed to be exhibited more widely by men.

Note the narrator's emphasis on the diversity of characters encountered in the Custom-House. He concludes: 'It contributes greatly towards a man's moral and intellectual health, to be brought into habits of companionship with individuals unlike himself, who care little for his pursuits, and whose sphere and abilities he must go out of himself to appreciate' (p. 25). Nathaniel Hawthorne is indicating the variousness of human beings, and suggesting the impossibility of containing the natures of all within a single frame, such as the Puritan structure of belief. The need for tolerance and understanding appears here as a commonsensical lesson to be derived from daily experience.

Nathaniel Hawthorne comments upon the strangeness of seeing his name, the sign, 'Nathaniel Hawthorne', not as before on the title-pages of books, but stamped onto packaging passing through the Custom-House. This seemingly incidental observation is actually central to the concern of *The Scarlet Letter* with the way in which signs change their meaning according to context. The letters that form his name have a shifting relationship to him as a living being, according to the conditions of their use. The name can identify an author, but it can also authorise the entry of goods through a port. Similarly, the scarlet 'A' which becomes associated with Hester Prynne does not contain her essence, but functions according to the framework of understanding in which it is perceived.

Nathaniel Hawthorne relates his discovery of the scarlet letter 'A'. It is offered as evidence, as material proof of the story which follows. Adopting a scientific approach to it, Nathaniel Hawthorne finds that each limb of the letter is three and a quarter inches in length. Yet while it leant itself to measurement, it did not readily yield its significance: 'Certainly, there was some deep meaning in it, most worthy of interpretation, and which, as it were, streamed forth from the mystic symbol, subtly communicating itself to my sensibilities, but evading the analysis of my mind' (p. 32). The point is that just as the author's name assumed significance according to context, so this portentous sign requires the telling of its tale to unleash the range of its potential meanings.

It is clear that the sign has meaning, but importantly for our reading of the book, that meaning is not self-evident. It lends itself to a range of interpretations. This is amply shown later, and is established firmly in this introductory chapter. Of Hester Prynne herself, we are told that she acted as nurse and counsellor to the community. The narrator allows comparable variation in the interpretation of her charitable acts. Some might have regarded them as an unwelcome intrusion, but many must have viewed this woman 'with the reverence due to an angel' (p. 32). Is that the real meaning of the 'A'?

As editor, Nathaniel Hawthorne asserts that the story which follows has the authority of historical account; it is not just rather the product of his creative imagination. Consequently, the story of Hester Prynne has a more general import; it has the moral gravity of a distillation from actual, recorded events. Yet while he establishes his claim for 'the authenticity of the outline' (p. 33), he concedes that he has developed the skeleton of the story through his invention.

The literariness of its rendering is immediately apparent; the patterning of image and vocabulary is carefully directed, in a way that would be inappropriate to the oral testimonies which are the supposed source of the story. The tone of 'The Scarlet Letter' is very different from the colloquial and conversational voice of 'The Custom-House', but while it mimics at times the grammar and vocabulary of seventeenth-century Boston, and while it works variations on **allegory**, an old literary mode, it is nonetheless recognisably a nineteenth-century composition. The importance of artistry in establishing a tenable moral position is asserted from this point on.

The editor's position allows Nathaniel Hawthorne to remark upon an earlier surveyor's impressive wig. Fashions had changed between Hester Prynne's day and that of Surveyor Pue, and had changed again between his day and Nathaniel Hawthorne's own. Outward signs may alter, but certain aspects of human behaviour remain constant. Nathaniel Hawthorne is interested in signification, but he is equally concerned with what endures. He recognises, however, that moral responses need to be modified to suit the different temper of the times.

He remarks that he worked on developing the story while pacing the floor, and this exercise produced an appetite for food. Nathaniel Hawthorne is insistent that thought should not be considered in isolation. The action of the intellect has to be viewed in relation to the processes of the physical body. The head should not be separated from the heart, and vice versa. That is one of the major arguments of this book.

The definition of **romance** offered here has become famous. It is analysed in some detail later in this note (see Text 1 in Textual Analysis), but it should be remarked that the definition, with its emphasis on a fusion of the Actual and the Imaginary, is another instance of Nathaniel Hawthorne's insistence that head and heart, fact and fiction need to be held in creative balance. The kind of book *The Scarlet Letter* is, its formal character, is entirely in keeping with its thematic concerns. This contributes a great deal to its aesthetic success.

Nathaniel Hawthorne moves on to suggest that the civil servant forfeits more of his creative resources the longer he relies upon the support of the post. After initial publication of the book, his critics accused him of indulging his personal bitterness here, following loss of office due to a change of government. But it is Nathaniel Hawthorne's point that the artist should serve 'in the united effort of mankind' (p. 38), and such a tenured post can dull one's sense of belonging to that effort. The safety and security of salaried work can create insensitivity through the weight of routine. Here Nathaniel Hawthorne seems in agreement with Emerson and Thoreau in their insistence upon 'self-reliance'. Like them, he describes himself as 'a man who felt it to be the best definition of happiness to live throughout the whole range of his faculties and sensibilities' (p. 39). In practice, however, he conducted his later life in a manner quite distinct from the Transcendentalists (see Literary Background).

By casting himself as a victim, prey to hostile officials, the narrator is creating a further link with that self-reliant woman who will be the focus of the following narrative. Referring to himself as subjected to the guillotine, he is placing himself in a situation comparable to Hester on the scaffold. But like Hester, Nathaniel Hawthorne claims to have made the most of his situation. Like her, he turned to art, and dedicated his energies to its proper execution, setting himself aside from the town and its affairs, although in distinctly more congenial surroundings than Hester was permitted by her fate. The agents of commerce will soon be forgotten, but, Nathaniel Hawthorne allows himself to envisage that his artistry will endure, and in doing so it will preserve the memory of the rebellious woman with whom he has in this way wedded his own fortunes.

The first time was three or four years since Nathaniel Hawthorne published an account of his Concord home, in *Mosses from an Old Manse* (1846)

"P. P., Clerk of this Parish" fictional author of a satirical memoir in the *Memoirs of Martinus Scriblerus*. Nathaniel Hawthorne's contemporaries attributed the piece, mistakenly, to Alexander Pope. Like Arthur Dimmesdale, P. P. has fathered a child out of wedlock

old King Derby Elias Hasket Derby (1739–99), a merchant whose vessel *Grand Turk* was the first from New England to reach China

the last war with England the 'War of 1812', concluded in December 1814

Matthew, at the receipt of custom one of Christ's disciples, described thus in his own Gospel – Matthew 9:9

slop-sellers sellers of clothing for sailors

Wapping here used generally for an area of dockland such as that specifically at Wapping in London

Loco-foco the term was a used disparagingly of members of the Democratic party. The name derived from a kind of match, which had enabled a meeting in 1835 to continue despite being plunged into darkness as a result of a practical joke

Gallows Hill the supposed site of the hanging of witches in 1692

New Guinea the part of Salem where immigrants from Southern Europe settled

that first ancestor Major William Hathorne (1607–81) arrived in Massachusetts in 1630, and immediately established himself as a prominent figure in the community

the President's commission Nathaniel Hawthorne served as Surveyor in Salem Custom House between 1846 and 1849. His appointment was authorised by President James K. Polk (1795–1849)

General Miller James F. Miller (1776–1851) rose to prominence during the War of 1812, and had been Collector for over two decades when Nathaniel Hawthorne joined the Custom-House

Whigs the Republican Party was formed during the 1850s; prior to that the opposition to the Democrats in the American political system were known as Whigs

Boreas in Greek mythology, the god of the North Wind

our common Uncle 'Uncle Sam', the popular personification of the United States

the elder Adams John Adams (1735–1826), President from 1797 until 1801. His son, John Quincy Adams (1767–1848) held that office from 1825 until 1829

Ticonderoga a fort beside Lake Champlain in New York State. The British took it from the French in 1759, and the Americans, led by Ethan Allen and Benedict Arnold, took it in 1775

Chippewa or Fort Erie American forces defeated the British at Chippewa on 5th July 1814. They occupied Fort Erie, over the Canadian border for several months

Brook Farm an idealistic communal project set up in 1841 at West Roxbury, nine miles from Boston, by George Ripley. Nathaniel Hawthorne was a member of the group for eight months, but grew increasingly sceptical

an intellect like Emerson's Ralph Waldo Emerson (1803–82) was the most influential American philosopher of the nineteenth century

Assabeth the Assabet (as it is now spelled) is one of the tributaries of the Concord River. Nathaniel Hawthorne went boating on the Assabet during his residence in Concord between 1842 and 1845

Ellery Channing the poet William Ellery Channing (1818–1901) was a friend of Thoreau and subsequently became his biographer

Thoreau Henry David Thoreau (1817–62) was a philosophical anarchist, closely associated with Emerson

Hillard's culture George Stillman Hillard (1808–79) was a Boston lawyer with literary inclinations, who became a close friend and supporter of Nathaniel Hawthorne

Longfellow Henry Wadsworth Longfellow (1807–82) was a poet, best remembered for 'Hiawatha'. Nathaniel Hawthorne met him while they were students at Bowdoin College

Alcott Amos Bronson Alcott (1799–1888) was a radically idealistic member of the Transcendentalist group. In 1843, he founded the short-lived 'Fruitlands', a Utopian community based on dietary reform

a pen like that of Burns or of Chaucer Robert Burns (1759–96), the Scottish poet, was an excise-officer at Dumfries from 1791. Geoffrey Chaucer (c.1343–1400), author of *The Canterbury Tales*, became Controller of the Customs in the Port of London in 1374

Billy Gray William Gray (1750–1825), a highly successful Salem merchant, who consequently became Lieutenant-Governor of Massachusetts

Simon Forrester Simon Forrester (1748–1823) was born in Cork, Ireland. His activities as a privateer made him extremely wealthy

'Change the Merchant's Exchange in Boston

Governor Shirley William Shirley (1694–1771) was Royal Governor of Massachusetts from 1741 until 1749, and from 1753 until 1756

Jonathan Pue *Felt's Annals* record that Pue became Surveyor at Salem in 1752

Felt's Annals Joseph B. Felt published *The Annals of Salem from its First Settlement* in 1827. A second edition appeared during the 1840s

'Main Street' this sketch by Nathaniel Hawthorne had appeared in Elizabeth Palmer Peabody's *Aesthetic Papers*, in 1849. The comments here suggest an intention to reprint the piece in this volume; it actually reappeared in the collection, *The Snow-Image* (1852)

the Essex Historical Society founded in 1821. Salem was located in Essex County, Massachusetts

General Taylor Zachary Taylor (1784–1850), a Whig, became President in 1849

Irving's Headless Horseman in the story 'The Legend of Sleepy Hollow' by Washington Irving, published in *The Sketch-Book* (1819–20)

The Town-Pump! Nathaniel Hawthorne published a sketch, 'A Rill from the Town-Pump', in 1835. It was collected in *Twice-Told Tales* (1837)

CHAPTER 1: THE PRISON-DOOR

The Boston prison-house, and the crowd which surrounds its door, are described

The citizens of Boston gather before the door of the town's prison. The narrator describes their dour appearance, and comments on the ugliness and aged look of the building. To one side of its door stands a beautiful wild-rose bush, a striking anomaly in this grim context.

After the lengthy 'Custom-House' preface, this opening chapter is strikingly brief. A different style and tone have been adopted, far more formal, and more portentous.

Nathaniel Hawthorne immediately and concisely establishes the nature of this New England community in the seventeenth century: male-dominated, sober, their religious devotion suggested through their 'steeple-crowned hats'. The firmness of their faith, but also the inflexibility of their morality, are conveyed through the oak and iron of the prison-door.

After the stern demeanour of place and people evoked in this opening paragraph, Nathaniel Hawthorne invokes the aspiration of America's early settlers towards attainment of an earthly paradise. Amongst Nathaniel Hawthorne's contemporaries, this dream was sustained in the writings of the Transcendentalists (see Literary Background).

Against such idealism, Nathaniel Hawthorne insists on the need for both a cemetery and a prison. These features are common to all human communities, and reveal the Fallen condition of human beings. Nathaniel Hawthorne espoused the Christian belief that the Original Sin, committed in the Garden of Eden, has resulted in our innate sinfulness. He shared this view with his Calvinist ancestors, but as *The Scarlet Letter* demonstrates, Nathaniel Hawthorne sought to use this as the basis for a compassionate view of our shared plight.

Popular rhetoric celebrated America as a New World, but Nathaniel Hawthorne's Boston, after only twenty years of its history, is far from boasting newness in its 'beetle-browed and gloomy front'. The conventional image of the New World was of a garden, modelled after the Eden itself, but here that is travestied through mention of weeds growing around the prison. The prison itself is conceived emblematically as 'the black flower of civilized society' (p. 45).

Flower imagery, was famously deployed by J. Hector St. John de Crèvecoeur, in his *Letters from an American Farmer* (1782), where early Americans were compared to plants regenerated by their transplantation to New World soil (see Literary Background). Nathaniel Hawthorne pursues this imagery further in the wild rose-bush growing beside the prison-door. In its sensual beauty it symbolises the ambivalent status of Hester Prynne and her transgression. It is beautiful, yet it is wild.

Nathaniel Hawthorne's aim in this book was to find an ethically viable middle way between the laws of Puritan Boston and the energies of Nature. By linking the rose-bush to an actual historical figure, Ann Hutchinson, Nathaniel Hawthorne, in accordance with his conception of **romance**, straddles both a broadly **symbolic** and a verifiably historical level of meaning, enriching both.

It is important to recognise that Nathaniel Hawthorne is setting his story in a highly stylised, essentially artificial landscape. The prison and the cemetery, on the one hand, and the rose-bush, on the other are symbols with a very obvious meaning. The prison stands for sin and the graveyard for death. The bush stands for natural beauty and wildness. This is crude symbolism, because it is too obvious. If that were all Nathaniel Hawthorne could manage, his work would scarcely merit our attention. But the fact that these symbols are so closely determined is part of his larger strategy in the book.

Soon we are to be introduced to Hester Prynne, who wears on her gown a scarlet letter 'A'. The fact that this symbol can assume other meanings than that which the Puritan magistrates intended is crucial to any responsive reading. We are virtually forced to make an identification of Hester Prynne with the wild rose, while the Puritans are aligned with jail and cemetery. But Nathaniel Hawthorne lures us into such simple reading in order to heighten our sense of the need for more flexible and sensitive interpretation as the story unfolds.

Cornhill now Washington Street, in the city of Boston, Massachusetts

Isaac Johnson's lot Johnson was one of the first settlers to arrive in Boston. He died in 1630, the year of settlement, leaving land for the establishment of a jail, a graveyard, and a church

King's Chapel New England's first Episcopalian church was the focus of sectarian discord, with Congregationalists arguing that there was no place for such a church in Massachusetts

Ann Hutchinson Ann Hutchinson (1591–1643) was exiled from Massachusetts in 1638, on account of her unorthodox religious beliefs. She moved to Rhode Island, and then to New York, where in 1643 she was killed by Indians. Hutchinson was an Antinomian, belonging to a sect which believed in intuitive disclosure of God's grace to individuals, without institutional mediation. Antinomians challenged civil law which, they said, had no authority over an individual's soul. In 1830, Nathaniel Hawthorne had published a sketch of 'Mrs Hutchinson', in which he had expressed his disapproval of such radicalism, and argued that total religious tolerance damaged the welfare of a community.

CHAPTER *2*: THE MARKET-PLACE

Hester Prynne is led from the Boston jail, carrying her baby. A scarlet letter 'A' is attached to the breast of her gown. She is displayed upon a platform in the market-place

The women in the crowd discuss the adulteress Hester Prynne, whose emergence from prison they await. The town-beadle appears, and is described as the embodiment of 'the whole dismal severity of the Puritanic code of law' (p. 49). Then a voluptuous, yet elegant, young woman appears, bearing a three-month old baby in her arms. On the breast of her gown she wears a scarlet letter 'A', which she has embroidered using rich thread. Members of the crowd make disparaging comments about her.

The beadle leads Hester to the market-place, where she is exhibited to public view, upon a kind of scaffold. The dignitaries of the town look on from a balcony. Hester is confronted with the general gravity, and is unable to escape intense and sombre observation.

Her mind ranges back to England, where she grew up. She envisages herself there, in company with a 'misshapen scholar' (p. 55). Before long, however, she is forced back to the realities of Boston, the market-place, and the stern crowd.

The narrator considers how people's character may be read from their appearance. The possibility of reading the depths of character from its surface is one of the book's major concerns.

An important guide to our interpretation of the story is provided by 'The Custom-House', which emphasises changes of emphasis in Massachusetts society between the early seventeenth and mid nineteenth century. Nathaniel Hawthorne is keen to show that values have been modified, and that such modification can continue.

The narrator notes the severity of the New England Puritan character. In Europe, Puritanism still had to define itself against Catholicism, and so it had to assert itself in a way that often seemed aggressively harsh. In America, other pressures were experienced by the emigrants establishing communities amid a hostile environment, with a multitude of unfamiliar challenges. But Nathaniel Hawthorne is highlighting the intolerance of this group, which journeyed to the New World largely to escape persecution.

The Boston community is theocratic; it is 'a people amongst whom religion and law were almost identical' (p. 47), and those who transgressed the law were consequently regarded as sinners who merited no sympathy, and were treated with severity. Nathaniel Hawthorne is building a critical picture of a society which he regards as too lacking in human warmth, although he will stop well short of sanctioning transgression of the law. It is the extremity of Puritan attitudes that he seeks to counter in this **romance**

Nathaniel Hawthorne's view was that women might exercise an ameliorative influence upon conventionally masculine social values, but the narrator notes an unwholesome curiosity towards punishment shown by Bostonian women. Nathaniel Hawthorne felt that many of the improvements in social attitudes may be identified with a gradual feminisation of behaviour. This involved a softening of attitudes, the extension of greater compassion to others, and increased sensitivity to suffering. Hester Prynne, by the end of *The Scarlet Letter*, has clearly become an agent for such beneficial change.

Nathaniel Hawthorne's contemporary Margaret Fuller argued that rather than being in exclusive opposition, qualities of masculinity and femininity were to be found in varying degrees in all men and women. Nathaniel Hawthorne appears to be espousing that view. His narrator refers to the 'man-like Elizabeth' (p. 48), who had ruled England from 1558 until 1603. It is pertinent to mention here that Fuller felt the New World would become a more moral place than Europe; Nathaniel Hawthorne might be suggesting that the severity of the Puritans was in part moral coarseness inherited from the Old World.

Significantly, it is from the point of view of the crowd that we first get to learn about Hester Prynne, and her adulterous transgression of communal and divine law. Before we encounter the key players directly we witness the cloud of opinion in which they and their actions are embedded. Interpretation and critical judgement, with which we as readers are involved inextricably, are enacted in the narration right from the start of the tale. Of course, at this point, Arthur Dimmesdale is still cast in a positive light; his guilt is not suspected. Interpretation can be mistaken; judgements can be wrong.

The discussion shifts to the scarlet letter, the stigma imposed on Hester by the magistrates. The rigidity of the Puritans' understanding meant that 'A' stood unequivocally for 'adulteress'. But as modern readers, we are conscious of how the meaning of signs can alter according to context. Indeed, by the end of the story the people of Boston are themselves conceiving other meanings to be attached to that letter.

The Scarlet Letter is an investigation of signification, of how we derive meanings from signs. Nathaniel Hawthorne is arguing that acknowledgement of a multiplicity of possible meanings, or **polysemy**, is preferable to perception of a single rigid meaning. This is not just an incidental linguistic preference; it lies at the heart of Nathaniel Hawthorne's moral position.

The Puritan community regarded all signs as having an absolute, divinely ordained significance. The leading men of that community are seen in *The Scarlet Letter* to assume that they have privileged understanding of God's intention, and so they control the way in which meaning is attributed to signs. The real drama of the story lies in the challenge posed by Hester Prynne's case to the authority of Puritan interpretation.

This does not mean that Nathaniel Hawthorne was challenging God. But he was demonstrating how the position assumed by the

New England theocrats conflicted with the moral and political conduct of a modern democratic society. American democracy involves many points of view, and it involves the potential for change. Both of those aspects of the political system which Nathaniel Hawthorne supported required that signs could be amenable to varying interpretations, depending upon where one stands and when.

To clarify this, we see in this chapter the town-beadle, carrying his official insignia, symbols of the power invested in him. He is himself to be read as a sign, an embodiment of 'the whole dismal severity of the Puritanic code of law' (p. 49). Seventeenth-century Bostonians would presumably have seen this figure as a proper and dignified **personification** of the law. Perception of his 'dismal severity' comes with a later, much more liberal understanding. Note that the beadle acts 'in the King's name' (p. 51), reminding us that the action occurs a century and a quarter before the founding of the modern American republic.

Nathaniel Hawthorne has already, at this point, got us into the habit of looking for signs, and of considering our options for interpretation. The process started in 'The Custom-House'. A momentum gathers, and as we continue to read we are constantly on the look-out for signs, constantly alert to the need to interpret. We share this inclination with the characters in the story and with the narrator, who now indulges in a further act of interpretation. Noting the 'impulse' which makes Hester clutch her baby to her breast, he suggests that this is less a maternal gesture than an instinctive attempt to conceal the token of her shame, the scarlet letter 'A' attached to her bodice. Should we accept this view?

'Impulse' is an important word in Nathaniel Hawthorne's work. It signifies that part of human beings which is closest to the life of animals, the drives of the body, the appetites and passions. But the narrative focus now shifts to Hester's lavish embellishment of the scarlet letter. This is a work of conscious artistry, a cultural artifact of the kind which clearly distinguishes human achievement from animal existence. Embroidery of the stigma is an important act of

defiance, and onlookers recognise it as such. It alters the appearance
of the letter, but it also opens up its meaning. It is not just a
negative sign, but has become a token of artistry. As we shall see
later, it is important that this 'A' might signify 'artist' as well as
'adulteress'.

Nonetheless, Hester is an adulteress; that is not to be denied. She
is described in a manner which stresses her sensuality and physical
attractiveness. It is vital that we see her sexual allure to be
sufficiently great to have led Minister Dimmesdale to follow his
passions, against the dictates of reason and law. He is a respected
theologian, but Biblical scholarship has not preserved him from the
weakness of Fallen humanity. This fact is an important element in
Nathaniel Hawthorne's challenge to the authority of the Puritan
leaders.

Note that Hester's 'lady-like' qualities are perceived as such in the
context of her time, according to 'the antique interpretation of the
term' (p. 50). Nathaniel Hawthorne is indicating how social
assumptions of all kinds are prone to change through time; this
is a key theme of *The Scarlet Letter*. In particular, he is suggesting
that 'feminine gentility' involved for his contemporaries greater
delicacy and grace than Hester possessed. Nathaniel Hawthorne
felt that this more gracious femininity had wrought significant
improvements in the way that American life was conducted in the
nineteenth century.

Boston in the seventeenth century was a frontier town, 'on the edge
of the Western wilderness' (p. 54). Although Nathaniel Hawthorne
insists that the town already bears the marks of age, this wilderness
was a constant reminder of the precariousness of a relatively new
community. That sense of danger was undoubtedly a factor that
resulted in the rigour of Puritan conduct.

In *The Scarlet Letter* the wilderness forms part of the **symbolic**
landscape of Nathaniel Hawthorne's **allegory**. It is where the 'black
man' roams, the incarnation of all that the community most feared
and sought to keep at bay through its strict adherence to the law.
We may see Hester's sensuality as a parallel to that wilderness, in

that it represented for the Puritans an untamed threat to reason. Remember that Hester has emigrated to Massachusetts. She grew up in Elizabethan England, in a long-established society, which had confidence in its way of life.

The beadle escorts Hester to a scaffold erected in the market-place, the public centre of Boston. The narrator remarks how the penal system in New England has altered over two hundred years, another instance of change in social custom. The essence of the old punishment was to expose the captive to the public gaze, prohibiting concealment of shame. Hester Prynne is accordingly put on display where the sign on her gown is visible to all.

It is worth noting that *The Scarlet Letter* is set at the time of the Civil War in England, which resulted in Charles I, the King whose authority is exercised by this beadle, being executed in full public view by the Puritans of old England, under Oliver Cromwell.

The narrator speculates that a Papist (Roman Catholic) in the crowd might have seen the Madonna and Child figured in the appearance of mother and baby. Of course, Nathaniel Hawthorne is being boldly **ironic** here, as a Papist would not have been tolerated amongst the Puritans. This speculation does, however, further his point that interpretations will vary according to one's time, place, or set of beliefs. It also reminds us of the doctrine of Original Sin which, as we shall see, underpins Nathaniel Hawthorne's moral understanding. Mary's conception with Christ was Immaculate, that is, untainted by the Fall, although Jesus entered the world to redeem Fallen humanity.

Hester's imagination furnishes some kind of defence against the leaden weight of reality. Nathaniel Hawthorne might here be seen to be developing the important thematic concern with personal and social necessity for art: 'Possibly, it was an instinctive device of her spirit, to relieve itself, by the exhibition of these phantasmagoric forms, from the cruel weight and hardness of the reality' (p. 54) (see Themes).

In her imagination she conjures figures from her past, including her father and mother, and an aging scholar, with power to read the human soul. This man is later disclosed to be Hester's husband, Roger Chillingworth. In keeping with the theme of artistry, these images are said to inhabit her 'memory's picture-gallery' (p. 55). At the end of the chapter, however, she is confronted with the inescapable reality of the market-place.

Note that in dialogue Nathaniel Hawthorne uses vocabulary in accordance with seventeenth-century usage (e.g. 'Marry, I trow not!' p. 48), creating an authentic period feel, while signalling another change in social custom, the difference in language over two centuries (see Language and Style). His narrative voice in 'The Custom-House' establishes an evidently colloquial, and welcoming nineteenth-century tone. If language has changed, then why should morality not also have developed to match the requirements of the age?

Mistress Hibbins Ann Hibbins, wife of a once prosperous Boston merchant, was hanged as a witch in 1656

the sumptuary regulations of the colony the Puritan community observed laws which forbade luxury in terms of clothing, or other worldly goods, and excesses of indulgence in terms of food and drink

CHAPTER 3: THE RECONGNITION

> Hester recognises a figure in the crowd. The stranger learns of Hester's adultery, and of the scarlet letter 'A' which she has been condemned to wear as a stigma. We are introduced to Arthur Dimmesdale. Hester refuses to disclose the name of her partner in adultery

Hester is an object of unremitting observation, but she herself sees a figure in the crowd whom she recognises. It is evident that his presence fills her with intense distress. This singular man, who is accompanied by an Indian, makes a sign for her to refrain from acknowledging him, and he in turn feigns ignorance of her to fellow onlookers.

A townsman tells him the accepted version of Hester's story, that her husband was a scholar in Amsterdam, who had sent her ahead to the New World and had not himself arrived. In the intervening period

Hester conceived and gave birth to a child. Hester has refused to name the father of the baby.

The stranger is told that the community's laws can punish such adulterous transgression with death, but the mercy of the magistrates has in this case arrived at a penalty of three hours exposure to the crowd, followed by a lifetime wearing the scarlet letter 'A' upon her breast, signifying that she is an adulteress. The stranger asserts that Hester's adulterous partner will in time be made known to the community.

The narrator shifts attention to a balcony overlooking the market-place, where Governor Bellingham watches the proceedings, in the company of other eminent figures, including the Reverend John Wilson and the Reverend Arthur Dimmesdale. Hester numbs herself against the onslaught from her persecutors, while her baby cries with agitation. She is interrogated, but defiantly refuses to disclose the name of her lover.

Note that the stranger, who is soon revealed to be Hester's husband, Roger Chillingworth, is also presented for interpretation. Throughout *The Scarlet Letter*, we are made aware of our interpretative acts, which place us in a comparable situation to the characters in the story. Here, we feel the need to discover this man's identity, and to understand his relationship with Hester, and we look for clues within the narrative. To begin with, there are 'unmistakable tokens' in his appearance to show that he has developed his intellectual powers to a high degree (p. 56). This, surely, is the same 'misshapen scholar' remembered by Hester in Chapter 2.

By having an onlooker recount Hester's story in brief to the stranger, Nathaniel Hawthorne shows how a point of view precedes interpretation of the facts of any case. His point is that no facts have a plain and simple existence which is self-explanatory. There is always an interpretative framework.

Governor Bellingham is one of a number of historical figures whom Nathaniel Hawthorne includes in his fiction. This device accentuates the dual nature of the work, as an imaginative work of fiction, and as a kind of historical document. It befits Nathaniel Hawthorne's conception of **romance**, that *The Scarlet*

Letter is a highly stylised and artificial variation upon **allegorical** convention, and yet is grounded in historical actuality.

Bellingham is also an emblem of the community, which significantly is indebted for its development 'not to the impulses of youth, but to the stern and tempered energies of manhood, and the sombre sagacity of age' (p. 59). We have already seen the word 'impulse' linked, as it will be on numerous further occasions, to Hester Prynne and her transgressive love-affair.

Boston is governed as a patriarchy; that is, it is ruled by men who adopt the role of fathers in relation to other members of the community. As we have seen, they are portrayed as singularly stern fathers, and the narrator notes their exceptional inappropriateness as judges of 'an erring woman's heart' (p. 60). In the case of John Wilson, it is noted that his kindheartedness was far less developed than his intellect, and was a matter of some shame to him. Here Nathaniel Hawthorne is directing our sympathy away from such figures, and towards the passionate Hester, in accordance with his broad distinction of head and heart as centres for motivation of human behaviour.

With **irony** that becomes glaringly apparent as the story develops, the young preacher Arthur Dimmesdale is required to admonish Hester to confess the identity of her partner in adultery. Nathaniel Hawthorne, as usual in his characterisation, pays careful attention to Dimmesdale's appearance, and to the nature of his response to circumstances as it can be read from his demeanour. The young preacher is characterised as unworldly to a degree that makes him seem almost childlike, for all his scholarly achievement. He does not seem to belong amongst the town's 'fathers', and yet he is, ironically, the unlawful father around whose identity the story revolves.

We saw that the wild rose-bush provided a link between Hester and the natural world, which exists beyond society's laws. A comparable image is tellingly evoked in the adjectives attributed to the minister's 'freshness, and fragrance, and dewy purity of thought' (p. 61). The narrator also notes Dimmesdale's blushing cheeks, a significant natural parallel to the scarlet token of Hester's transgression. Such clues are present from the start of the tale, and if we are capable of shrewd detective-work we should be able to start building a revealing picture as we read on. A major piece of evidence is signalled through the baby's outstretched arms, disclosing an instinctual attraction to her natural father.

Hester's public humiliation is one of a series of dramatic scenes that carry the dynamic of Nathaniel Hawthorne's narrative. These are interspersed with commentary on the nature of the characters, on their historical context, and on moral issues raised by the story (see Narrative Techniques and Structure).

Note that Hester assumes the role of sacrificial victim, willingly assuming the burden of her partner's sin and subsequent punishment. Her selfless loyalty is testimony to the strength of her love. The stylisation of the narrative does not make it easy for Nathaniel Hawthorne to convey the couple's love for one another in a way that engages our sympathy. But it is important for our interpretation of events that we have a sense of the genuine devotion shown by Hester. Her refusal to speak may be read as comment upon the fact that as a woman she has been deprived of a suitable voice in a patriarchal society.

John Wilson speaks of the symbolic letter in such a manner as to colour it in the imagination of his audience so that it 'seemed to derive its scarlet hue from the flames of the infernal pit' (p. 63). The role of imagination in human understanding is stressed with the chapter's final observation that 'it was whispered, by those peered after her, that the scarlet letter threw a lurid gleam along the dark passage-way of the interior' (p. 64). The important point being made here is that meaning is accrued to the sign through its contextualisation. Wilson has located the letter within a structure of interpretation that makes it appear infernal. Another context might create an entirely different mode of interpretation. The significance derived here is not an inherent quality of this piece of cloth in the shape of 'A'.

the Daniel who shall expound it the prophet Daniel is seen in the Biblical book that bears his name to have been an accomplished solver of riddles. Notably, he deciphered the writing on the wall at Belshazzar's feast. His skill as an interpreter makes the reference particularly apt to Nathaniel Hawthorne's romance

Governor Bellingham Richard Bellingham (1592–1672) was a lawyer, born in Lincolnshire. He departed from England in 1634, became governor of Massachusetts in 1641, and subsequently served in the office on two further occasions

John Wilson John Wilson (1591–1667) was an English preacher, who arrived in Boston in 1630. He led the opposition to Ann Hutchinson, defending the authority of the Church against the Antinomians

CHAPTER 4: THE INTERVIEW

> **Back in the prison, Hester is attended by a physician. He is the strange figure from the market-place. Hester promises not to disclose that he is, in fact, her husband, Roger Chillingworth. Chillingworth vows to discover the identity of her lover**

Returned to prison following her ordeal of public scrutiny, Hester continues to be watched, ostensibly in order to prevent her harming herself or her child. A physician is brought to attend her: it is Roger Chillingworth, the stranger from the market-place. He administers medicine, and alleviates the baby's condition. He then turns his attention to the mother.

We learn that Chillingworth and Hester Prynne are legally husband and wife. Like the magistrates, Chillingworth is keen to discover the identity of the father of Hester's child, a man who, he feels, has wronged them both. He is insistent that he will find the culprit, and insists that his own identity as her husband should remain concealed. She takes an oath, and they enter into a pact of secrecy.

> Note that the baby, in its distress, is described as 'a forcible type, in its little frame, of the moral agony which Hester Prynne had borne throughout the day' (p. 65). 'Type' is used here to mean a sign or symbol. We might say that the infant is seen here as a **personification** of Hester's inner turmoil.

Chillingworth straddles the worlds of medieval alchemy and modern science, which was making advances during the seventeenth century. It is in keeping with the practices of modern science that Chillingworth conducts extensive researches based on close observation. We may recognise in his behaviour a resemblance to those detectives, who in later fiction have adapted the methods of science in order to assist the workings of law.

There is evident **ambivalence** in his attitude to Hester: he wants to restore her health, but takes satisfaction in the prospect of her subsequently bearing the badge of shame throughout her life. Again, Nathaniel Hawthorne is indicating the difficulty of interpreting motive. Chillingworth does 'all that humanity, or principle, or, if it so were, a refined cruelty, impelled him to do' (p. 68). Hester herself is unsure how to read him. She remarks that his 'acts are like mercy', but she tells him, 'thy words interpret thee as a terror' (p. 69).

Chillingworth does make generous acknowledgement that his unsuitable marriage to Hester was an act of folly, and is at the root of the dilemma in which she finds herself. But that does not prevent his hunger for vengeance. The dramatic consequence of marriage between partners of disparate ages has provided material for many writers, including Geoffrey Chaucer in 'The Merchant's Tale' (late fourteenth century), and George Elliot in *Middlemarch* (1871–2). In this case, it is possible that Nathaniel Hawthorne has a larger issue in mind. We may consider reading this marriage as a parallel to the combination of European traditions and a New World environment in the settlement of America. The inappropriateness of that political and cultural 'marriage' resulted in the Declaration of Independence in 1776. Is Hester's 'A', then, America?

Master Brackett this was actually the name of Boston's jailer at the time. Nathaniel Hawthorne derived this and other historical details from Caleb Snow's *History of Boston*

I know not Lethe nor Nepenthe in Greek mythology, Lethe was a river in the underworld, whose waters caused loss of memory. Nepenthe was a drug, used by the Egyptians to eliminate pain and anxiety

Paracelsus Paracelsus was the pseudonym of Philippus Aureolus
Theophrastus Bombastus ab Hohenheim (1493–1541), a renowned Swiss
alchemist and astrologer, who was Professor of physics and surgery at Basel
University

the Black Man that haunts the forest the Puritans tended to identify forests
with the Devil, known popularly as the Black Man

CHAPTER 5: HESTER AT HER NEEDLE

> Hester is released from the jail. She takes up residence on
> the outskirts of the town, and supports herself and her
> child through needlecraft

Hester's imprisonment ends. She takes up residence in an abandoned
cottage, built on sterile ground at the sea's edge, on the outskirts of
the community. There, children, innocent of the cause of her isolation,
spy on her as she performs needlework, which increasingly absorbs her
time and energy. In addition to work she dutifully performs for the town's
officials, the compassionate Hester also makes clothing for the poor.

There is little action to advance the plot in this chapter; rather it
develops through the narrator's commentary the characterisation of
Hester Prynne, indicating the complexity of her response to the simple,
yet dreadful penalty imposed upon her.

With characteristically dramatic use of contrast, Nathaniel
Hawthorne stages Hester's release from jail in bright sunshine. This
sunshine does not appear affirmative to her, however, as it makes
her more acutely aware of the scarlet letter on her breast. Again,
the pain of exposure to public view is stressed. So is the sense that
her stigmatisation will be her daily fate, with no abatement
foreseeable.

Hester envisages that she will become 'the general symbol at
which the preacher and moralist might point, and in which
they might vivify and embody their images of women's frailty
and sinful passion' (p. 71). In other words, she will lose her
individual identity, and become a 'type' (we have already seen this
happening momentarily in the case of her baby). She will become
'the figure, the body, the reality of sin' (p. 72). Nathaniel

Hawthorne uses such crude symbolism throughout this story, but we are guided to recognise its inadequacy. Nathaniel Hawthorne's reductive employment of characters as symbols is intended to show us that human complexity requires a more subtle mode of understanding.

Explaining why Hester remains in the community that no longer imposes any physical restraints upon her, the narrator again deploys with **irony** the familiar imagery of plants: 'Her sin, her ignominy, were the roots which she had struck into the soil' (p. 72). These roots are also figured as a binding chain. Later, Nathaniel Hawthorne will turn that image into a positive one, revealing the chain that links human beings to be our shared fallibility and imperfection. The image of the chain then becomes the basis for more sensitive moral discrimination. Note that the transformation of this image from negative to positive parallels the fate of the scarlet letter itself. In both cases, the meaning of a **symbol**, or sign, is seen to be susceptible to fundamental change; it is not anchored inextricably in a single authoritative interpretation.

Hester's cottage by the sea draws attention once more to the highly stylised landscape in which Nathaniel Hawthorne sets his tale. It has all the artificiality of a theatrical set, heavily laden with symbolic resonance. In fact, it resembles the topography of classic **allegory**, such as we meet in Edmund Spenser's *The Faerie Queene* (1590, 1596). Nathaniel Hawthorne greatly admired that poem, and in fact named his daughter Una, after the figure in it who stands for Truth. But remember that he is using such devices to show the limitations of classic allegory, which attributed a fixed and unequivocal meaning to its symbols.

As we have noted, the scarlet letter is crucially modified by Hester's embroidered embellishments. In this chapter we are told of her needlecraft, which in practical terms enabled her to make enough money to survive, but, beyond that, it developed into the practice of artistry. Feminist critics have subsequently appreciated Nathaniel Hawthorne's point that this was a vital art 'then, as now, almost the only one within a woman's grasp' (p. 74). It was the silent woman's means of expression.

It also reflects upon Nathaniel Hawthorne's own practice. He noted in 'The Custom-House' that his Puritan ancestors would have found it shocking that he should work as a writer. In 1850, eminently practical Americans were still largely unsure about the worth of artistic endeavours.

By embroidering the letter on her breast, Hester has conferred upon it an aesthetic value, modifying its functional significance. Here in miniature is the effect gained in **romance** – the starkly utilitarian, or routinely familiar is transformed by the moonbeams (as it were) of artistry. It becomes 'a specimen of her delicate and imaginative skill' (p. 74) (see Text 1 in Textual Analysis). Nathaniel Hawthorne's essential argument in this book is that art can establish a richly beneficial middle course between the arid stringency of the intellect, and the potentially damaging excesses of the passions.

Hester otherwise dresses with notable plainness, but she has altered the letter, intervened in the production of meaning, and re-defined the token of moral law. The colony's sumptuary laws preclude popular indulgence in such ornamental work, but the leading figures in Boston had a taste for ornamentation of their tokens of office, and their ceremonial clothing. This taste seems to show a telling inconsistency in their behaviour, and elsewhere in the tale Nathaniel Hawthorne comments upon the vestiges of Elizabethan indulgence to be detected amid the Puritanical chasteness of New England.

It may be that Nathaniel Hawthorne was enjoying a private joke when he wrote of Hester's services to the town dignitaries. His own rise to office in the Salem Custom-House came about through exercise of his writing skills in service of a particular political faction. Indeed, when that group lost power, he lost office. He reserved his real skill, however, for his own elaboration of *The Scarlet Letter*.

the brow of Cain a reference to Genesis 4:15, 'And the Lord put a mark on Cain, lest any who came upon him should kill him'

CHAPTER 6: PEARL

Hester's daughter, Pearl, is characterised as she starts to grow up

The narrator shifts attention from the mother to her child. Pearl is portrayed as a wild, lawless infant, almost uncontrollable in her reckless energy. Hester watches her with anxious concern, in case the child's appearance or behaviour should reveal the secret of her father's identity.

Hester muses on what has been transmitted to her child from her own turbulent spirit during the unsettling time of her pregnancy. Pearl is capricious and impulsive, but her attention returns repeatedly to the scarlet letter. We are told of Hester's sensitivity on catching her daughter gazing at the token of her shame with a disarming smile upon her face, which Hester feels inclined to interpret in the least comforting of terms. The child amuses herself by throwing wild flowers at the scarlet letter.

The name, Pearl, is another example of an overdetermined sign; that is, one which allows no variability in interpretation. We inevitably recognise a reference to a precious object, produced by the introduction of an impurity, and developed in secret. We must learn to read Pearl as other than just a symbol.

But, she is also couched in the imagery of plant and garden, being described as 'a lovely and immortal flower', bred 'out of the rank luxuriance of a guilty passion' (p. 80). In her ornamented clothing, she is presented as the incarnation of the scarlet letter, a living stigma. Yet importantly she is described as various and mutable. She does not lend herself to a single definition: 'in this one child there were many children, comprehending the full scope between the wild-flower prettiness of a peasant-baby, and the pomp, in little, of an infant princess' (p. 81).

Pearl is not to be pinned down, and, by analogy, nor is the scarlet letter. It may seem to have a definitive meaning, but it is in the nature of signs to be **polysemous**, to have multiple meanings. Just as a letter of the alphabet stands in arbitrary relationship to the world in which it functions as a sign, so Pearl's nature 'lacked reference and adaptation to the world into which she was born' (p. 81). Of course, letters come to participate in socially agreed meanings, and similarly Pearl, as she grows, must enter into some form of social framework. She cannot remain wild, but nor should she be too rigidly constrained.

She has inherited her mother's faculty of imagination, although without the mature discipline manifested in Hester's needlecraft it appears in more sinister light: 'The unlikeliest materials, a stick, a bunch of rags, a flower, were the puppets of Pearl's witchcraft' (p. 84). Her imagination allows her to transform reality. This is the essential attribute of the artist, especially the writer of romance. The child's lawlessness, however, results in creation of hostile figures, images of 'an adverse world' (pp. 85–6). It is necessary for Pearl to become socialised, if her creativity is to be directed to more constructive ends. Still, it appears to be Nathaniel Hawthorne's understanding that it is the fate of any artist to remain, like Hester, on the margins of social life.

With overt **irony**, the narrator remarks that Pearl manifests such physical perfection that she might be deemed 'worthy to have been brought forth in Eden; worthy to have been left there, to be the plaything of the angels, after the world's first parents were driven out' (p. 80). It might be argued that Hester actually emphasises the child's Fallen nature by adorning her in rich fabrics, remote from the naked innocence of the prelapsarian Garden of Eden.

It was a commonplace amongst early writers on America to compare it to Eden, and to see the continent as an opportunity for human beings to regain paradise on earth. Amongst Nathaniel Hawthorne's contemporaries, the Transcendentalists cherished faith in the ability of men and women to attain perfection akin to that of Adam and Eve before the Fall (see Literary Background).

Nathaniel Hawthorne came to consider such Utopian idealism to be dangerous and irresponsible. He became deeply committed to the view that this world had no place for Edenic perfection. His view was that it is only by acknowledging our common failings that we can achieve a compassionate and tolerant moral understanding of other human beings. American democracy was not, Nathaniel Hawthorne recognised, a perfect society. But he believed it did have the potential to be the most enlightened society to date.

This chapter is very much concerned with transmission of characteristics from one generation to the next. Nathaniel Hawthorne felt that history shapes the present, and that we need to learn from its examples in order to make appropriate modifications. He deplored the insistence of Ralph Waldo Emerson that life could be conducted as if individuals and societies had no past. For Nathaniel Hawthorne the historical dimension was a moral necessity.

The narrator remarks upon the more severe conduct of family life in Puritan New England, with children being regulated far more rigidly than in the mid nineteenth century. This is another example of Nathaniel Hawthorne offering a historical perspective in which a more liberal spirit is seen to be emerging with the passage of time.

Hester's imagination, sensitised by her public shaming and private anxieties, insistently sees Roger Chillingworth looking out from the child's eyes, as though he possessed the infant's spirit. Pearl asks her mother to tell her where she came from, and it seems as if Chillingworth is actually driving her to detect the identity of her father.

Hester is disturbed by the gossip of townsfolk, who in the absence of a known father choose to designate Pearl 'a demon offspring' (p. 88). This kind of attribution, the narrator observes was found in Roman Catholic societies of medieval Europe, and Martin Luther, the Protestant reformer received such a designation. He observes ironically that such attributions were by no means unknown amongst New England's Puritans, the inheritors of Luther's rebellious faith. Nathaniel Hawthorne repeatedly discloses the inconsistencies of the Puritans in order to challenge the authority of the coherent world-view which underpinned their rigid system of interpretation.

Pearl in the Gospel of Matthew 13:45–6 there is a parable of a merchant who sells all that he has in order to buy 'one pearl of great price'. There is also a well-known medieval English allegorical poem called 'The Pearl'
sowing broadcast the dragon's teeth in Greek myth, Cadmus kills a dragon, then sows its teeth. They grow into armed warriors, who fight amongst themselves until only five remain
Luther Martin Luther (1483–1546) the leading figure in the Reformation in Germany. His revision of Christianity argued that salvation was to be won by faith rather than works

CHAPTER 7: THE GOVERNOR'S HALL

Hester and Pearl deliver gloves to the Governor's mansion

The narrator tells of an occasion when Hester, accompanied by Pearl, visited Governor Bellingham at his mansion, in order to deliver a pair of embroidered gloves, but also to pre-empt a proposal amongst the townsfolk to deprive her of custody of the child.

On the way, the couple encounter local children, who fling mud at them. The governor's mansion, which was then a new building, is described. It is decorated according to the taste of the age, and it belies somewhat the sombre character of the Puritans. Turning to the garden, Pearl asks for a red rose, but the flower is denied to her by her mother.

A group of dignitaries approaches them.

It is reiterated here that Pearl, in her richly decorated clothing is to be seen as 'the scarlet letter in another form; the scarlet letter endowed with life!'. Indeed, it is acknowledged that Hester has 'carefully wrought out the similitude' (p. 90). She loves her child, of course, and by consolidating the identification of Pearl with the stigma, she appears to have found a way to come to terms with her punishment.

In his description of the Governor's mansion, Nathaniel Hawthorne again indicates how the New World inherited tastes and attitudes and practices from Europe. This contributes to the larger theme of inheritance (see Themes). Among these practices is that of keeping servants. The depiction of Bellingham's house highlights the stratified nature of this community, which Nathaniel Hawthorne would have seen as morally inferior to the a modern republic which in 1776 had undergone a revolution against the injustices of the old ways.

Significantly, the inherited social practice is signified through clothing: 'The serf wore the blue coat, which was the customary garb of serving-men at that period, and long before, in the old hereditary halls of England' (p. 92). It is not only Hester who is differentiated by coloured cloth. Bellingham's own continuity with the English past is signalled through his taste for beer, and through the portraits tracing his familial lineage.

Note the strikingly conceived image in which Hester's reflection in the breastplate of the Governor's suit of armour is grotesquely distorted, effectively concealing the woman behind the scarlet letter. Nathaniel Hawthorne is using the breastplate **metonymically** to indicate those patriarchal, martial values which have diminished Hester Prynne's humanity, and in its place has located this potent stigma.

It is observed that the English taste for ornamental gardening has been superseded here by practical cultivation in unpromising, hard soil. So much for Eden regained!

selectmen elected officers who managed the public affairs of Boston

the right of property in a pig in 1644 the legislative assembly was divided into two distinct houses

a seven years' slave Nathaniel Hawthorne is referring to the practice of indentured service. English people who wished to emigrate to the New World, but could not afford the passage often committed themselves to a period of servitude to a wealthy individual who could pay for their crossing. Nathaniel Hawthorne is signalling the fundamentally undemocratic nature of Puritan society

the Chronicles of England Raphael Holinshed's *Chronicles of England, Scotland and Ireland* (1577), now best remembered as a source book for Shakespeare's plays

the Pequod war the Pequod were an Indian tribe inhabiting south-eastern Connecticut. They entered into conflict with European settlers in 1633, and skirmishes continued until 1637, when an English militia decimated them

Bacon, Coke, Noye, and Finch Sir Francis Bacon (1561–1626), Sir Edward Coke (1552–1634), William Noye (1577–1634), Sir John Finch (1584–1660), all notable figures in British legal history

the Reverend Mr. Blackstone reputedly the first settler on the Boston peninsula, Blackstone, an Episcopalian, had no taste for the Puritans who followed, and is said to have joined the Indians instead

CHAPTER 8: THE ELF-CHILD AND THE MINISTER

Governor Bellingham tells Hester that Pearl may be taken from her. John Wilson, Arthur Dimmesdale and Roger Chillingworth are also present. Hester addresses to Dimmesdale a special plea that she should be allowed to keep her child. Pearl holds Dimmesdale's hand, and he kisses her forehead

Governor Bellingham is described. The old man is accompanied by John Wilson, Arthur Dimmesdale and Roger Chillingworth, who has been attending to the young minister's flagging health. Hester observes that her husband has grown uglier and 'duskier' (p. 99), suggesting further corruption or his moral self.

Bellingham compares Pearl to a red rose. He then confronts Hester with the possibility that the child will be taken from her. Wilson, the old minister, tests Pearl with regard to her Christian upbringing. Hester has trained Pearl in an orthodox manner but, apparently through some innate perversity, she refuses to answer correctly.

The Governor is appalled at the three-year-old's ignorance. Hester makes passionate defence of her position, arguing that Pearl is her source of happiness, but that her presence is simultaneously a form of torture. She implores Dimmesdale for assistance, and he makes special, and successful, pleading for her 'instinctive knowledge' of the child's requirements (p. 101).

Pearl caresses Dimmesdale's hand with unaccustomed tenderness. He responds by kissing her brow.

The narrator cites a tale that Governor Bellingham's sister, Mistress Hibbins, tried after this meeting to entice Hester to join a company of witches in the forest. Hester is said to have rebuffed the suggestion triumphantly.

The description of Bellingham continues to suggest that despite his society's professed rejection of luxury and indulgence, a taste for the good things life has to offer persists in private behaviour. Such duplicity should have a bearing on our sense of Dimmesdale's culpability in living a double life.

Pearl's response to the Reverend Wilson is a blatant instance of Nathaniel Hawthorne's strategic overdetermination of the meaning of signs. She declares that 'she had not been made at all, but had been plucked by her mother off the bush of wild roses, that grew by the prison-door' (p. 99). Pearl's character becomes further stylized; the image of the rose becomes more emphatically central to the text's overt meaning. But at the same time, Nathaniel Hawthorne is preparing us to resist such facile correspondence between symbol and interpretation.

The tenderness displayed between Pearl and Dimmesdale is to be read as an instinctive mutuality, reminding us of the actual identity of father and daughter.

The tale of Mistress Hibbins, indeed the presence of that curious old woman throughout the story, is a significant chink in the Puritan armour. For all the rigorous assertion of social coherence, it is clear that Boston contains wild elements that complicate our sense of the community's real nature.

The narrator raises the possibility that the story of Mistress Hibbins, which may be authentic, might also be read as a parable. **Parable**, like **allegory**, is a form of overdetermined narrative, in which the intended meaning is closely delimited and controlled. It is that kind of narrative which *The Scarlet Letter* aims to prise apart, in order to introduce a healthy plurality of meaning.

old King James's time James I was on the throne of England from 1603 until 1629

the Lord of Misrule a master of revelry, who held dominion during the Christmas festivities. He was often accompanied by mischievous children, and was frowned upon by the Puritans

a worthy type of her of Babylon! the narrator refers to Revelation 17:3–5: 'I saw a woman sitting on a scarlet beast which was full of blasphemous names, and it had seven heads and ten horns. The woman was arrayed in purple and scarlet, and bedecked with gold and jewels and pearls, holding in her hand a golden cup full of abominations and the impurities of her fornication; and on her forehead was written a name of mystery: "Babylon the great, mother of harlots and of earth's abominations"'

the New England Primer the first edition of this book of instruction was published in 1690. It contained the basic components of literacy, combined with essentials of faith, such as the Lord's Prayer and the Catechism

the Westminster Catechism the Westminster Assembly of Divines published the Shorter and Longer Catechisms in 1647. It used a question and answer format to elucidate Calvinist doctrine

the tithing-men elected officers, responsible for maintaining public order

CHAPTER 9: THE LEECH

Roger Chillingworth is characterised. His relationship with Dimmesdale is described

As its title indicates, this chapter develops the characterisation of the physician, beginning with a reminder that Roger Chillingworth is an assumed name, concealing his real identity. The narrator muses on the rarity of religious zeal amongst members of the medical profession.

Chillingworth's close association with Dimmesdale is noted. The high public regard in which the minister is held is stressed. Ironically, his illness is taken by some members of his congregation as an indication that the world is not good enough for him. His own view is that he is not worthy of life. The minister's characteristic gesture, a tell-tale sign, is to place his hand over his heart. The mysterious arrival of Chillingworth is generally regarded as an act of Providence, and is read by some as offering a miraculous cure for the ailing minister's seemingly terminal condition.

Chillingworth has studied Dimmesdale and has discovered that his character involves an active amalgam of thought and imagination; in other words, the head is refined, but so is the heart, and they contest to determine his behaviour.

At the contrivance of their friends, the two men come to lodge together, at the house of a local widow. Their apartments are described. The narrator remarks with evident **irony** that this seemed the best option for Dimmesdale, given his evident resistance to the idea of marriage.

It is increasingly disclosed that not all Bostonians think so well of the physician. Indeed, in some quarters he is identified as an agent of Satan. No wonder that Dimmesdale is beset by 'gloom and terror' (p. 112)!

The title of this chapter, 'The Leech', is an old name given to physicians, on account of their practice of using leeches to draw blood from patients. Medical science had made considerable advances by the time Nathaniel Hawthorne was writing, so he is suggesting another area of human activity in which evident improvements had occurred since the seventeenth century.

The term has a further significance here, because it so aptly describes the parasitical way in which Chillingworth clings to Dimmesdale, drawing sustaining energy from his host and depleting Dimmesdale's own resources.

The fact that Roger Chillingworth is a pseudonym, assumed to conceal his real identity, presents another form of duplicity following that identified in the last chapter. It also conforms to the story's general concern with the problematic relationship between signs and their supposed referents.

The narrator makes an unusually bold claim for the power of intuitive understanding: 'When an uninstructed multitude attempts to see with its eyes, it is exceedingly apt to be deceived. When, however, it forms its judgement, as it usually does, on the intuitions of its great and warm heart, the conclusions thus attained are often so profound and so unerring, as to possess the character of truths supernaturally received' (p. 111). This affirmation might be seen to endorse a democratic ideal as the true political and moral expression of a people's feelings, but the declaration is not to be read in such a straightforward fashion.

Critically, at this point, some of the townsfolk have begun to recognise a sinister quality in Chillingworth, which is even tinged (like the scarlet letter itself) with the infernal. His appearance s then read as that of 'Satan's emissary' (p. 112). What appeared initially as universal consensus, now seems fraught with contradiction. In one brief chapter, Nathaniel Hawthorne has shown how members of the Puritan community could endorse views of this man which range across the spectrum of conceivable characterisations, from God's gift to 'diabolical agent'. He is once again effectively undermining the authority of the claims on which the community founds its judgements.

the Elixir of Life this remarkable solution was said to transmute base metals into gold, and to offer a cure for all human ailments. This dream of the alchemists fascinated Nathaniel Hawthorne

Sir Kenelm Digby Sir Kenelm Digby (1603–65) was an adventurer, diplomat, alchemist, astrologer, scientist and philosopher. He discovered that oxygen was necessary for the growth of plants. Nathaniel Hawthorne read his *Private Memoirs* (published in 1827)

the New Jerusalem refers to Revelation 21:2: 'And I saw the holy city, new Jerusalem, coming down out of heaven from God'

the Gobelin looms members of the Gobelin family were clothmakers, based in Paris from the fifteenth century. Their tapestries were considered the finest in Europe

David and Bathsheba in 2 Samuel 11–12, Bathsheba was the wife of Uriah the Hittite. David deliberately sent Uriah to his death in battle, so that he might advance his seduction of Bathsheba

Nathan the Prophet Nathan was sent by God to register his displeasure with David's self-centred actions

Sir Thomas Overbury Thomas Overbury (1581–1613) was poisoned in the Tower of London, following his opposition to the marriage of his patron, the Earl of Rochester, to the Countess of Essex

Doctor Forman Simon Forman (1552–1611) was a quack doctor, who lived in Lambeth, London. He left letters at his death which in 1615 implicated him in trial of the Countess of Essex

CHAPTER 10: THE LEECH AND HIS PATIENT

Further description of Chillingworth's obsessive interest in Dimmesdale. The physician discovers why the minister repeatedly places his hand upon his own breast

This chapter extends the concerns of the last. Chillingworth, once a morally upright man, has developed an obsession with Dimmesdale's secret life that occasions comparison not only with a miner but also with a grave-robber.

The leech has herbs, unfamiliar to both men, which he says he gathered in the graveyard, where they grew upon the heart of a man who had guarded a guilty secret. This initiates a revealing discussion between the two men. Chillingworth's application of the intellect to unpack the secrets of the soul is countered by Dimmesdale's faith that God alone has access to such secrets, and sits in absolute judgement of them. The men, from their opposing points of view, debate the pros and cons of revealing secret guilt. Dimmesdale suggests that Hester's overt guilt is easier to bear than hidden sinfulness.

Their conversation is interrupted by Pearl's laughter, heard from the graveyard. The child dances upon a gravestone. She responds to her mother's entreaties to stop by attaching burrs, from the plant burdock, to the contours of the scarlet letter.

The men turn their conversation to Pearl. Chillingworth asks whether any discernible principle governs the child's behaviour; Dimmesdale replies, that it is only 'the freedom of a broken law' (p. 117). Pearl casts a burr at the Minister, who evades it. She then identifies Chillingworth with the Black Man, and suggests he has ensnared Dimmesdale.

Dimmesdale reiterates that a physician should concern himself with the body alone, and that sickness of the soul can be dealt with only by God. Then, in a panic, he rushes from the room. The rift between the men is soon healed, but Chillingworth is committed to probing that 'strange sympathy betwixt soul and body' which he discerns in the minister (p. 120). He intends to investigate the psychosomatic symptoms Dimmesdale displays.

Soon afterwards, he chances upon Dimmesdale sleeping in a chair, and takes the opportunity to examine the place on his chest to which the minister's hand repeatedly moves. The physician makes a discovery which causes him to respond dramatically, with a mixture of diabolic triumph and wonderment.

Chillingworth's obsessive prying into Dimmesdale's inner life is for Nathaniel Hawthorne the Unpardonable Sin, a violation of the individual soul which no human being has the right to perpetrate. This is the theme of a number of Nathaniel Hawthorne's most powerful short stories, including 'Ethan Brand' (see Nathaniel Hawthorne's Other Works). It is clear that had he lived to witness psychoanalysis, Nathaniel Hawthorne would have deplored the practice.

Note that Chillingworth concludes that Dimmesdale has 'inherited a strong animal nature from his father or his mother' (p. 113). Not only does this fit with the theme of the incongruity of surface and substance, with Dimmesdale's scholarly appearance belying his passionate nature, but it also continues the thematic concern with inheritance (see Themes). Behind this concern lurks Original Sin, the primal legacy of Adam and Eve, which provides a common bond between us all. It seems particularly significant, then, that Chillingworth is compared to a thief, and the minister to a man jealously guarding a personal possession which is 'the apple of his eye' (p. 114).

Pearl's dance upon a gravestone shows not just lack of respect for the dead, but lack of awareness of, and concern for, the past. The image conveys Nathaniel Hawthorne's view of the irresponsibility of Emerson and his Transcendentalist followers (see Literary Background). Nathaniel Hawthorne was insistent that human beings require a strong sense of the continuities between the past and the present.

Pearl is described as being divorced from the past, in a manner which inescapably recalls the rhetoric of America's brave New World: 'It was as if she had been made afresh, out of new elements, and must perforce be permitted to live her own life, and be a law unto herself, without her eccentricities being reckoned to her for a crime' (p. 118). In *Letters from an American Farmer* (1782),

Crèvecoeur wrote of the American as a new man, following a new mode of life, and acting upon new principles, entertaining new ideas and new opinions.

Nathaniel Hawthorne can only follow this line to a limited degree. He did believe that America was in general morally superior to Europe, but Pearl is too wild. Her insights must be contained by a mature sensitivity to others; but she certainly does have insights. After tracing the scarlet 'A' with burrs, she throws one at Dimmesdale, as if to implicate him in her mother's crime. She then compares Chillingworth to the Black Man, the devil who dwells in the forest; she is not alone in perceiving in him a Satanic presence.

Bunyan's awful door-way in John Bunyan's *Pilgrim's Progress* (1678), a door which opened onto one of roads to Hell. It was reserved for hypocrites and those who betrayed God's trust

CHAPTER 11 : THE INTERIOR OF A HEART

We learn of the physical scourging Dimmesdale inflicts upon his body, and of the mental and emotional anguish he endures. It is evident that the minister is in fact Pearl's father

The action remains suspended, while Nathaniel Hawthorne pursues further the moral nuances of the relationship between the two men. Chillingworth becomes 'not a spectator only, but a chief actor, in the poor minister's interior world' (p. 122).

The chapter also considers Dimmesdale's status amongst fellow ministers, and his standing in the community more generally. We are granted insight into the workings of his mind, as he longs to tell the community of his sinfulness, and to dispel the lie he has been living. He is painfully aware that a general confession of guilt, not specifying the particulars of his transgression, would confirm for his congregation his relative saintliness; his listeners would direct their attention to their own sinfulness.

Dimmesdale scourges his own body. He also subjects his body to extreme fasting, and prolonged periods without sleep. By staring into a mirror, he 'typified the constant introspection wherewith he tortured, but could not purify, himself' (p. 127). He has visions of demons and angels, of deceased friends, of his parents, and of Hester with Pearl. As the chapter ends, this anguished figure leaves his chamber under the cloak of night.

> Nathaniel Hawthorne has provided sufficient clues for readers to be left in no doubt that Dimmesdale is Pearl's father, so the evaluations of him by fellow citizens which we encounter here appear intensely **ironic**. These estimations also serve to foreground the pressures which generate his profound moral unease. Not only is he concealing his guilt, but he is held is unusually high regard; that makes his situation all the more difficult to face.

> A third-person narration is sustained, but we are granted insight into the operations of the minister's tormented consciousness. We also learn that he flagellates himself, after the fashion of those fanatics of medieval Roman Catholicism who punished their bodies in order to show their contempt for this world, and their dedication to the next. Note the regularity of Nathaniel Hawthorne's invocations of Roman Catholicism to describe the practices of these New England Puritans. He seems to be saying that just as American society in many ways manifests the legacy of Europe, so the practical religion of these radical Protestants retains obvious elements of the older form of Christian belief.

> His efforts to mortify his body produce hallucinatory visions. The terrain of **romance**, which Nathaniel Hawthorne has mapped out in this book, lends itself perfectly to this tortured form of imagination. The minister could 'discern substances through their misty lack of substance, and convince himself that they were not solid in their nature', yet he sensed that, nonetheless, these visions were actually 'the truest and most substantial things' in his life (p. 127). The techniques of romance enable Nathaniel Hawthorne to show most effectively that 'To the untrue man, the whole universe is false' (p. 127).

the sanctity of Enoch Genesis 5:24: 'Enoch walked with God; and he was not; for God took him'. Enoch's closeness to God was such that he was transferred to Heaven without physical death

CHAPTER 12: THE MINISTER'S VIGIL

Dimmesdale mounts the scaffold in the market-place, in the depths of night. He sees a gleaming letter 'A' in the sky. He is joined by Hester and Pearl. Chillingworth arrives, and escorts the minister home. Next day, Dimmesdale delivers a particularly powerful sermon

As if sleepwalking, Dimmesdale mounts the scaffold where Hester Prynne stood exposed to public view seven years before. The difference is clear – the minister's exposure is under cover of darkness, and the market-place is deserted: 'There was no peril of discovery' (p. 129). Yet, he is overtaken by a sense that the entire world is looking at a scarlet token upon his breast.

He shrieks aloud, but despite causing some unrest in the Governor's house, with Mistress Hibbins showing a predictable interest, the cry passes generally unnoticed. Then, a light emerges from the darkness, carried by the Reverend Mr Wilson, returning from the deathbed of Governor Winthrop. The old man passes by, oblivious to the presence of the younger minister.

Dimmesdale laughs at a grotesque vision of being discovered conjured by his distressed imagination, and in response he hears Pearl laughing. The child is accompanied by her mother, who has also been attendant at Winthrop's demise, and has been entrusted with preparing the funereal robe.

Hester and her daughter join the minister on the platform, and united in their guilt, but also in their love, 'The three formed an electric chain' (p. 134). Pearl requests that he join them there at noon the next day. The minister prefers to defer that moment until God's Day of Judgement.

The portentousness of this encounter is amplified by a celestial event, a gleaming light in the sky, of a kind that the Puritans were accustomed to interpret as a sign from God. Nathaniel Hawthorne offers us the wisdom of a later age, whose faith had shifted towards scientific explanation, when he suggests that a meteor was the cause.

The immediate dramatic effect of the illumination is that the three figures are cast into light akin to that of midday. Chillingworth arrives.

Dimmesdale, for so long a close companion of the physician, declares that he hates him, and asks who he really is. Hester, alert to her vow, remains characteristically silent. Pearl, however, offers to cast light on the man, but only whispers childish gibberish. Chillingworth, who has also been administering to Governor Winthrop, asserts friendship and offers to escort the distressed minister to his home. Dimmesdale complies.

The next day is the Sabbath, and Dimmesdale delivers a sermon which is held to be of exceptional quality. At its conclusion, a sexton presents him with a glove, which he had left upon the scaffold, although the sexton is quick to attribute its appearance there to Satan's teasing intervention. He refers to the portentous sign seen on the night before. Dimmesdale denies seeing the letter in the sky.

This is an important chapter in both thematic and technical terms. It is a dramatic set-piece involving the heightened **symbolism** of **allegory**, but Nathaniel Hawthorne transforms that symbolism into a projection of an unsettled imagination. In doing so, he follows the lead of **Romantic** writers, such as Samuel Taylor Coleridge in 'The Rime of the Ancient Mariner' (1798), but he also advances his romance towards the territory later occupied by works of **psychological realism**.

The image of the 'electric chain' that binds the three figures on the scaffold is a transformation of the earlier image of the chain that binds Hester to Boston. This is a vital, living image of human beings united in their fallibility. In his story 'Ethan Brand' (1851), Nathaniel Hawthorne similarly refers to 'the magnetic chain of humanity'.

The suggestion that a meteor was the cause of the celestial light, which appeared to Dimmesdale as an accusatory 'A', is further measure of the distance between seventeenth- and nineteenth-century understanding. We should not merely take the latterday explanation as a higher authority, however. Nathaniel Hawthorne is indicating how a socially accepted framework for comprehension always conditions our point of view, and provides us with a context for interpretation. The narrator concentrates upon the psychological effect wrought by a natural phenomenon in combination with an agitated imagination.

Occurring in the depths of night, the effect of the illumination takes us again into the realm of **romance**, with its mode of unfamiliar disclosure. The town appears 'with a singularity of aspect that seemed to give another moral interpretation to the things of this world than they had ever borne before' (p. 135) (see Text 2 in Textual Analysis). Chillingworth's arrival, heightens the **Gothic** effect of the scene.

A sexton returns the minister's glove, found on the public scaffold. We recognise the consummate irony in the church officer's assertion: 'A pure hand needs no glove to cover it!'. He then speaks of the previous night's portent: 'A great red letter in the sky, – the letter A, – which we interpret to stand for Angel' (p. 138). This letter, seen in so different a light from that on Hester's breast, is viewed as a token that God had accepted Governor Winthrop into Heaven. Nathaniel Hawthorne is showing how signs are read differently according to the assumed context, even though they may be identical in form. The capacity of the sign to be **polysemous** is made clear, even as the resistance of the Puritans to multiple meanings is confirmed.

Governor Winthrop John Winthrop (1588–1649) was a successful lawyer, who became one of the founders, in 1630, of the Massachusetts Bay Colony. He was elected governor before he arrived in the New World, and was returned to that office in 1631, 1632, and 1633. His *Journal*, furnishes an invaluable account of the early years of this community, and testifies to an anti-democratic spirit amongst the early leaders. Nathaniel Hawthorne sets the scene in early May, although Winthrop actually died in March

Geneva cloak Geneva was the city of John Calvin, and ministers of the faith which took his name habitually wore black cloaks

CHAPTER 13: ANOTHER VIEW OF HESTER

> **Pearl is now seven years old. Hester has lost her physical attractiveness, but has become reconciled to her life as an outcast. The people of Boston have increasingly come to respect her abilities. Hester muses on Pearl's wildness, her own lot, and the fate of women more generally. Mother and daughter encounter Chillingworth**

Pearl is now seven years old – time passes in this Fallen world.

The narrator registers Hester's shock at the physically and spiritually depleted condition in which she found Dimmesdale. The rest of the chapter is devoted to a close consideration of the developments which have occurred in Hester's character.

Boston has grown used to the figure of Hester, and has come, paradoxically, to accept her in her outcast condition. The scarlet letter starts to become subject to other interpretations, with a distinctively positive slant.

Nonetheless, Hester has lost her physical attractiveness, the allure that contributed to initiation of her troubles, and she appears a passionless creature, cold and self-contained. The activity of her mind, in isolation from emotional sustenance, has resulted in a state of desperation. The route from this impasse of despair lies through compassionate assistance to another; in this case, Arthur Dimmesdale.

She determines to act in order to save him from Chillingworth's venomous interest. She assumes full culpability for enabling the physician to sustain proximity to the minister, with his true identity concealed. But she believes that her isolation has strengthened her for the task ahead, just as Chillingworth's vengefulness has diminished his powers.

The chapter ends with a fortuitous encounter between Hester and Pearl walking, and Roger Chillingworth collecting herbs.

> Nathaniel Hawthorne again invokes the image of a chain connecting all human beings, but in this case the bond is solely between the guilty couple: 'The links that united her to the rest of human kind – links of flowers, or silk, or gold, or whatever the material – had all been broken. Here was the iron link of mutual crime, which neither he nor she could break. Like all other ties, it

brought along with it its obligations' (p. 139). The relationship of individual rights and social obligations is one of the major concerns of the book (see Themes).

Hester's selfless generosity has been noted by the townspeople; she gives, but avoids taking. The sufferings of others enable her to enter their company: 'There glimmered the embroidered letter, with comfort in its unearthly ray. Elsewhere the token of sin, it was the taper of the sick-chamber' (p. 140). Again, the strangely illuminated terrain of **romance** enables us to perceive the **ambivalence** of the stigma, and so detect the moral complexities of Hester's situation, which are not perceptible under the daylight regime of Puritan patriarchal law.

The grip of a single, closely determined meaning for the scarlet letter 'A' weakens accordingly, within the community itself: 'Such helpfulness was found in her, – so much power to do, and power to sympathize, – that many people refused to interpret the scarlet A by its original signification. They said it meant Able; so strong was Hester Prynne, with a woman's strength' (p. 141). The token of her weakness is coming to appear the index of her ability as a compassionate human being amongst other human beings.

It takes longer for Hester to break through the 'iron framework of reasoning' that characterises the rulers of the community (p. 141). But it seems to be her very distinctiveness, the fact that she is not merely a type, that transforms Hester from outcast into 'our Hester, – the town's own Hester'. The scarlet letter then comes to impart 'a kind of sacredness' quite contrary to the intention behind its initial application (p. 142). Indeed, it becomes, in popular gossip, a kind of protective amulet, warding off physical as well as spiritual threats to Hester's person. The fact that she has broken out from the stereotype of the 'scarlet woman', that narrow classification, and has revealed her full humanity, means that the sign on her breast has to be reconsidered, and viewed in greater richness of meaning.

Hester has, nonetheless, lost her passionate aspect. The narrator observes that 'Much of the marble coldness of Hester's impression was to be attributed to the circumstance that her life had turned, in great measure, from passion and feeling, to thought' (p. 143). This conforms to Nathaniel Hawthorne's clear division of the realms of head and heart, and his insistence that to adhere to one pole to the detriment of the other results in an imbalance that jeopardises the individual as a whole. He valued art as a vital means to reconcile the two.

Hester has suffered an imbalance. The narrator notes that 'The world's law was no law for her mind' (p. 143), adding that her intellectual lawlessness, taking her far beyond the pale of socially acceptable thought, was not out of keeping with an age that was marked generally by intellectual turbulence. So, 'Men of the sword had overthrown nobles and kings', referring to the contemporary English Civil War, while scientists and philosophers were busy formulating new models to understand reality itself.

In her 'freedom of speculation' (p. 143), Hester is in accord with the spirit of the age, in Europe, rather than New England. To her Puritan countrymen this would have been a sin far beyond that emblematised by the scarlet 'A'. The narrator himself speculates that if she had not been restrained by her responsibility for Pearl, Hester would surely have followed the example of Ann Hutchinson, and founded a religious sect, or otherwise have acted to undermine the orthodoxies of the Puritan establishment.

Hester's musings extend to the lot of women generally, and whether their existence was itself justified by the scope of social functions they were permitted to perform. Nathaniel Hawthorne introduces aspects of the feminist debate that was being conducted by some of his more radical contemporaries, including Margaret Fuller, author of *Woman in the Nineteenth Century* (1845). Nathaniel Hawthorne seems to echo Fuller in the programme for reform which Hester envisages: 'As a first step, the whole system of society is to be torn down, and built up anew. Then, the very nature of the opposite sex, or its long hereditary habit, which has become like nature, is to be essentially modified, before woman can be allowed to assume what seems a fair and suitable position. Finally, all other duties being obviated, woman cannot take advantage of these preliminary reforms, until she herself shall have undergone a still mightier change; in which, perhaps, the ethereal essence wherein she has her truest life, will be found to have evaporated' (p. 144).

Nathaniel Hawthorne was not in favour of such concerted rebelliousness, and he would have considered that the practical responsibilities of motherhood exerted a necessary softening influence upon Hester's intellectual boldness. However, Pearl's wayward behaviour, her elfin impulsiveness, causes consternation in Hester's mind about the legacy of lawlessness she has apparently bequeathed to the child. She must free herself from 'the dark labyrinth of mind' (p. 145). In her frustration she even contemplates killing Pearl as an act of mercy, and then committing suicide. The narrator concludes: 'The scarlet letter had not done its office' (p. 145). Another mode of justice is required.

CHAPTER 14: HESTER AND THE PHYSICIAN

Hester engages in intense conversation with Chillingworth, while Pearl plays beside the sea

After sending Pearl to play at the water's edge, Hester enters into intense discussion with Chillingworth. He reports that the magistrates have debated removal of her stigma. She proudly retorts that its removal does not reside with the magistrates, and that it will fall from her of its own accord when the time is right.

She notes a sinister change in Chillingworth's appearance. They discuss Dimmesdale and the torment he has undergone. Chillingworth observes that he also has undergone undesired transformation, from a mild and scholarly man to a fiend in human form.

Hester declares to him her resolution to break her vow and reveal his real identity as her legal husband. She blames herself for the ruin of both men; but Chillingworth is still able to blame the inappropriateness of their marriage for the lamentable sequence of events.

The old man instructs Hester to deal with the Minister as she will.

Chillingworth's news that the magistrates are considering removal of the scarlet letter from Hester's breast shows that the iron framework of patriarchal judgement has been breached with the passage of time. But Hester's response reveals that she does not consider herself subject to Puritan law. She trusts rather to the integrity of her own moral sense.

The narrator suggests that the physician has transformed himself into a devil through seven years devotion 'to the constant analysis of a heart full of torture' (p. 148). Of course, the transformation is not conceived literally. Rather, Chillingworth has been possessed by an obsession. As previously noted Nathaniel Hawthorne considered this violation of another individual's soul to be the Unpardonable Sin, and it forms the theme of several of his short stories, notably 'Ethan Brand' (1851). Brand becomes a fiend 'from the moment that his moral nature had ceased to keep the pace of improvement with his intellect' (see Nathaniel Hawthorne's Other Works).

Chillingworth's readiness to concede his own folly in marrying inappropriately, and so initiating a disastrous course of events, appears to be to his credit. He is actually restating the view, which takes numerous forms in this book, that we cannot afford to ignore history. Nathaniel Hawthorne would argue that human beings must accept the legacy of past decisions and actions, before they can learn how best to deal with their consequences in the present.

But the physician does not allow much scope for individuals to control their own destiny in his doom-laden pronouncement that, 'it has all been a dark necessity. Ye that have wronged me are not sinful, save in a kind of typical illusion; neither am I fiend-like, who have snatched a fiend's office from his hands. It is our fate. Let the black flower blossom as it may!' (p. 152). America was a concerted attempt to evade the 'dark necessity' of history. Nathaniel Hawthorne sustained faith that it could do so, within limits.

CHAPTER 15: HESTER AND PEARL

> **Chillingworth leaves to collect herbs. Hester discusses with Pearl the significance of the scarlet letter on her gown**

Chillingworth leaves Hester with Pearl and continues to collect herbs. Hester meditates on the traces that Chillingworth might leave in his wake, like the tell-tale signs of pestilence. She has come to hate him, and views her past with him, and the fact of their marriage with amazement and dismay.

In the course of her play Pearl has constructed an 'A', formed from fresh green plants, to wear upon her own breast. Mother and child discuss the significance of 'A'. But Hester draws back from explaining to the seven-year-old the intended meaning of the stigma. In preserving Pearl's innocence in this matter, she feels that she has been false to the letter, for the first time. Pearl, however, is not satisfied with the evasion, and persists with her teasing questions.

> Pearl, at play, manifests an extraordinary imaginative faculty, which has clearly been inherited from her mother, and which she uses to transform the familiar environment into a world of wonder. In this she might be seen to parallel the writer of **romance**, although it is clear that Nathaniel Hawthorne considers the child to have inadequate grounding in routine reality. As usual, in conversation with her mother, Pearl manifests a disarming intuitive knowingness, but the limits to her knowledge correspond to the limits of her awareness of the realities of society and its laws.

> Hester recognises that, in spite of her continued wildness, her daughter is growing towards sympathetic companionship, and she discerns that her lawless exuberance might yet be socialised in ways that produce 'a noble woman' (p. 157). This actually transpires; at the end of the story we recognise that Hester has read correctly.

CHAPTER 16: A FOREST WALK

> **Hester and Pearl walk in the forest. They see Dimmesdale, evidently unwell, approaching along the forest track**

Hester remains resolved to apprise Dimmesdale of Chillingworth's real identity as soon as a suitable opportunity arises. She and Pearl approach the forest.

Pearl requests a story about the 'Black Man', living in the forest, of whom she has heard an elderly woman talk. The woman identified the scarlet letter as the mark of the 'Black Man', left upon Hester Prynne following her midnight meetings with him. Against such superstitious gossip, Hester refers Pearl to her own experience: she has never awoken to find her mother absent from her side, so how can that accusation be true? She does, however, concede that she did once meet that 'Black Man', and that the scarlet 'A' is, indeed, his legacy.

The minister approaches and, before being sent off to play once more, Pearl comments upon the way that he holds his hand upon his heart. She asks why Dimmesdale does not wear the token of his encounter with the Black Man where it is visible to all, as her mother does. While Pearl picks flowers, Hester returns to the forest track, prepared to confront the minister, who advances, obviously enfeebled.

> The action shifts to 'the primeval forest', less a realistic feature than **symbolic** topography of the kind to be found in classic **allegory**, such as Spenser's *The Faerie Queene* (1590). Indeed, Hester reads the setting allegorically; the forest 'imaged not amiss the moral wilderness in which she had long been wandering' (p. ·159). Nathaniel Hawthorne makes symbolic use of the play of sunshine through the pervasive gloom: Pearl is able to stand in sunlight, but at her mother's approach gloom descends, enabling Pearl to continue her teasing.

> This sequence is typical of the bold stylisation which Nathaniel Hawthorne deploys to convince us momentarily that we are actually reading allegory. At the same time he is invariably coaxing us to feel dissatisfaction at such crude signification, and directing us to look for more complex meanings.

> Pearl is said to lack 'the disease of sadness, which almost all children, in these latter days, inherit, with the scrofula, from the troubles of their ancestors' (pp. 160–1). Previously, we have seen the comparison between the seventeenth and the nineteenth century to judge in favour of the latter, with its general softening of attitudes and amelioration of conditions of social life. It comes as a surprise, then, to encounter this reference to increased sadness amongst children. But in the broader view, this also is a change for the good.

The point is that a sense of our mutual fate as Fallen beings arises when we learn to sympathise with the suffering of others. Such sympathy often arises from our own experience of suffering. That, rather than some abstract or idealised bond, is what links humanity, in Nathaniel Hawthorne's view. His essential moral position is that unalloyed happiness is ultimately as undesirable as unalloyed misery. Pearl's buoyancy imparts 'a hard, metallic lustre to the child's character', and she needs 'a grief that should deeply touch her, and thus humanize and make her capable of sympathy' (p. 161).

The 'Black Man' is a denizen of the allegorical landscape. He is a version of the Devil, and has distinct sexual connotations. Hester's admission of an encounter with him is a veiled allusion to her sexual transgression with Dimmesdale. As a child, Pearl has no means to comprehend the significance of this figure, and Hester, unable to offer helpful explanation, tries to divert her daughter from further inquiry.

She is repeatedly sent off to play when her mother wishes to converse with another adult on issues that seem to lie beyond the child's range of understanding. But, as noted earlier, Pearl has a disarming capacity for intuitive moral insight, which is demonstrated again here, in relation to Dimmesdale's habitual placing of his hand over his heart.

Once more, we see Pearl picking flowers, her little figure forming a striking contrast to that of Chillingworth, who is regularly glimpsed gathering herbs.

the Apostle Eliot John Eliot (1604–90) arrived in New England in 1630. In 1646, he began preaching to the Indians. During the 1660s he completed a translation of the Bible into Indian language

scrofula a tubercular condition, affecting the lymphatic glands

CHAPTER 17: THE PASTOR AND HIS PARISHIONER

Hester and the minister talk in the shadow of the forest. She discloses the truth about Chillingworth. Hester proposes that they should depart for the Old World, seeking refuge there. Dimmesdale declares that he cannot leave, but must remain to die in Boston

Gradually, Hester and Dimmesdale come to establish terms for frank discussion of their mutual plight. Both concede they have found no peace, but exist in a state of torment.

Dimmesdale, significantly, has 'laughed, in bitterness and agony of heart, at the contrast between what I seem and what I am!' (p. 167). He considers Hester fortunate in having her guilt displayed, rather than left to fester in concealment.

Hester affirms her continuing friendship towards her partner in sin. The narrator states plainly that Hester still loves Dimmesdale, passionately. But she is now compelled from within to disclose the devastating fact that Chillingworth is her husband.

After the initial shock, the minister manages to forgive Hester for this deception. He suggests that their own transgression seems minor by comparison with that committed by Chillingworth: 'He has violated, in cold blood, the sanctity of a human heart'. The couple agree that their unlawful act had 'a consecration of its own' (p. 170), and seated on the mossy trunk of a fallen tree, they hold hands. They linger in the gloomy forest, where Dimmesdale can at last be truthful.

Hester insists that the minister must escape from Chillingworth's gaze, either into the depths of the forest, or across the sea to the refuge of the Old World. Their flight would be not only from the obsessive physician, but also from the 'iron men' of Puritan Boston, with whom, she argues, the minister has little in common (p. 172).

But Dimmesdale insists that he must remain where Providence has ordained that he should spend his days, and that he should continue to aspire to help others, despite his sense of unworthiness. He says he will die alone; Hester counters that prediction with the assurance that he will not be alone.

The encounter of the minister and his former lover on the forest-track is described as comparable to that of two spirits 'in the world beyond the grave' (p. 165). The mention of ghostly apparitions in the definition of **romance** offered in 'The Custom-House' is echoed, with especial resonance.

Beyond the physical boundaries of social regulation, they have entered at last 'the same sphere' of existence (p. 166). It is a place where the couple are able to disclose to one another the inner turmoil they are experiencing. Dimmesdale argues that Chillingworth's violation of 'the sanctity of a human heart' (p. 170) is a greater sin than their own. As noted previously, such violation was, for Nathaniel Hawthorne, the Unpardonable Sin.

Although the affirmation by this couple that their love-affair has a sanctity of its own is consoling, it is delusory. They are attempting to isolate the relationship from its social and historical context, and while that is possible as long as they remain in the forest, it will prove untenable on their return to Boston. Although they have temporarily assumed the status of figures in a romance landscape, soon they will resume their social existence, alongside historical personages, such as Governor Bellingham.

There is lasting value, however, in the fact that Hester is seen to be 'exercising a magnetic power' over Dimmesdale's flagging spirit. Regularly in his fiction, Nathaniel Hawthorne uses images drawn from scientific study of electro-magnetism in order to evoke attachments between human beings which have no evident physical reality. In this case it is emblematic of the human capacity for mutual sympathy and awareness of a common fate.

Hester now advocates flight from Roger Chillingworth, and from Boston society more generally. Her sense of mutuality is here limited to an isolated relationship. Dimmesdale is not only being more realistic, but is morally superior, in Nathaniel Hawthorne's view, in his determination to remain and help others. The point is that he *does* have much in common with those Puritan 'iron men', although the manners of the day may accentuate differences. Nathaniel Hawthorne is not interested solely in an isolated experience of reciprocated feeling; he is concerned with the development of more tolerant and compassionate social groups.

Note the **irony** in Hester's suggestion that the couple flee to the Old World. This reversal of the dynamic of emigration to America is a graphic declaration that the New World is not paradise regained.

CHAPTER 18: A FLOOD OF SUNSHINE

Hester's isolation has developed her critical faculty and her rebellious spirit. Dimmesdale is inspired by her vision, and determines after all to escape to Europe with her. Hester removes and casts away the scarlet letter. She decides that the minister must be properly introduced to his daughter

The narrator comments upon the radical nature of Hester's isolation from the community: 'Her intellect and heart had their home, as it were, in desert places, where she roamed as freely as the wild Indian in his woods' (p. 174).

Dimmesdale, contrastingly, has remained steeped in the law of which he is a leading representative. Nonetheless, he is persuaded to change his mind, and makes the fateful decision to flee the community; such a declaration of his own guilt now seems preferable to perpetuating a duplicitous existence. He anticipates that they will make a clean break with the past, and in celebration of that prospect, Hester tears the symbolic letter from her breast. It falls beside a brook. Hester is immediately revitalised.

In her new enthusiasm, Hester is keen to introduce Dimmesdale to his daughter. Pearl has been playing amongst the wild creatures of the forest. The narrator suggests that 'the mother-forest, and these wild things which it nourished, all recognized a kindred wildness in the human child' (p. 178). Once again we see the child gathering flowers, an inverse image of the grotesque Chillingworth. She adorns herself with them, sharing Hester's taste and talent for embellishment, and comes to resemble the sprites of ancient myth, rather than a child of modern society. She approaches them slowly, wary of the minister.

Throughout the book, we have seen Hester persecuted, yet performing acts of care and compassion towards the people of

Boston. Dimmesdale, however, has remained a paragon in the eyes of the community, while entrapped in self-obsession. Yet at the end of the previous chapter, we saw Hester suggesting flight, while Dimmesdale resisted the temptation.

This chapter insists on the necessity of a social context for individuals. Dimmesdale is embedded in Boston, however uncomfortably; Hester, on the margins of the community, has been effectively ostracised. The effects of this isolation are now examined in further detail.

From her position as outsider, Hester has become an incisive critic of Puritan society and its institutions, 'criticizing all with hardly more reverence than the Indian would feel for the clerical band, the judicial robe, the pillory, the gallows, the fireside, or the church'. Note that the focus here is upon signs which customarily focus power and effect social cohesion. But these emblems of social regulation have no sanctity for Hester. She has become, in effect a dissident reader, who has come to reject orthodox interpretation and has created an alternative fabric of meaning.

The key point is, of course, that signs are susceptible to variant, or heterodox, reading, and although the Puritans may regard their symbols as having absolute meaning, signification is never absolute. It is always possible to find a point of view which will allow an alternative reading. Such readings form the social function of the critic, and it is that role, as well as that of artist, which Hester has now assumed.

In that sense her punishment, her isolation, has in fact been a form of liberation: 'The tendency of her fate and fortune had been to set her free. The scarlet letter was her passport into regions where other women dared not tread' (p. 174). She has been set free to see differently, and to think otherwise. Hester can be seen here as a representative of emergent feminism. What appeared to be an effective stigma, from one point of view, has turned out to be a means to slip through the restrictive net of accepted social values.

But note that Nathaniel Hawthorne does not endorse radical criticism for its own sake; he strongly disapproved of Margaret Fuller's more extreme proposals, for example. Rather, he saw that critical detachment assists beneficial processes of social change. If one is immersed in the habitual ways of a group it becomes difficult to recognise its flaws and shortcomings. Standing to one side, it becomes possible to identify areas where improvements are required.

Following removal of the scarlet letter, Hester is charged with renewed life. The narrator asserts that this change in her person registers 'the sympathy of Nature – that wild, heathen Nature of the forest, never subjugated by human law, nor illumined by higher truth' (p. 177). This is the thrill of lawlessness, rather than a benign communion with the natural world. We are in the primeval forest where the 'Black Man' roams, not the Edenic garden, and these illicit lovers are remote from the unfallen Adam and Eve.

Human beings live in cultures, not in nature. Pearl is shown amongst the wild creatures, but she is not an animal, and eventually she will have to learn to become a member of a society regulated by customs, laws and moral standards. More immediately, the forest is not a context within which her parents can long remain.

CHAPTER 19: THE CHILD AT BROOK-SIDE

Pearl approaches, and returns the scarlet letter to her mother, insisting that she must wear it. It is clear that the child will withhold her affection from the minister until he admits his guilt. The couple remain resolved to take flight for the Old World

The parents discuss their daughter, as she approaches them. Hester is full of praise for Pearl; Dimmesdale is concerned that her appearance might disclose the identity of her father. He takes comfort from her resemblance to her mother.

Hester's new-found happiness is fundamentally challenged by the child's refusal to recognise her. Pearl insists that her mother should wear the letter. With its return comes 'a sense of inevitable doom' (p. 184). But the anguish of this is mollified by Pearl's exhibition of a rare tenderness towards her mother. The minister persists in concealing his guilt, so Pearl withholds her affection. She washes the imprint of his kiss from her brow. The couple cling to their dream of escape.

The minister anticipates meeting Pearl with a mixture of eagerness and dread. Nathaniel Hawthorne emphasises that emotional responses rarely have the clarity of differentiation found in civil law or socially recognised moral distinctions.

The little girl has been spoken of earlier as an incarnation of the scarlet letter. Now, as she approaches her parents, the narrator observes: 'In her was visible the tie that united them. She had been offered to the world, these seven years past, as the living hieroglyphic, in which was revealed the secret they so darkly sought to hide, – all written in this symbol, – all plainly manifest, – had there been a prophet or magician skilled to read the character of flame!' (p. 180). Two major concerns of the book are continued here: inheritance, or transmission from one generation to the next, and reading the world as a structure of signs.

The comparison of Pearl to a flame is evocative; in the consciousness of Puritan New England, it would surely have figured as an emblem of infernal fire; to a later generation, it might appear as a flame of creative energy. Point of view is crucial to the interpretation of any sign. Nathaniel Hawthorne invokes the skill of prophet and magician to interpret with accuracy. These are figures from an earlier epoch; in a modern democracy, like Nathaniel Hawthorne's America, such privileged readers of signs are scarcely conceivable. But note that at the end of the tale, Hester clings to the vision of a redeeming prophetess.

The narrator asserts that 'Pearl was the oneness of their being' (p. 180). Perhaps Nathaniel Hawthorne was here consciously imitating the so-called **conceits** of the English poets, known as the **Metaphysicals**, who were contemporary with Hester Prynne and Dimmesdale. In 1633, John Donne famously wrote of a flea which, in drawing blood from two lovers, became the living emblem of the love that conjoined them. Pearl seems just such another emblem, and in terms of conventional morality she is not far less surprising a choice to figure love.

Note how Nathaniel Hawthorne's use of lighting in his staging of this important scene produces the **ambivalence** of **romance** despite the fact that the sun is shining brightly. He refers to Pearl's reflection in the brook in a way that dematerialises her physical body, and transforms her again into an elfin child: "'I have a strange fancy,' observed the sensitive minister, "that this brook is the boundary between two worlds, and that thou canst never meet thy Pearl again. Or is she an elfish spirit, who, as the legends of our childhood taught us, is forbidden to cross a running stream?"' (p. 182).

Ironically, Pearl, this creature who seems to exist beyond the pale of moral discrimination, now acts as a focus for the distinction of right and wrong. She does so above all by the fact of her existence, the inescapable fact of historical reality, which, as Nathaniel Hawthorne insists, must always weigh heavily upon the present. Her existence in itself must remind the couple of their transgression. In attempting to behave as if they are no longer answerable for their actions, the parents are effectively denying their child's existence.

Hester clings to her dream of escape in terms which suggest the potent dream that fuelled the settlement of America: 'I must bear its torture yet a little longer, – only a few days longer, – until we shall have left this region, and look back hither as to the land we have dreamed of. The forest cannot hide it! The mid-ocean shall take it from my hand, and swallow it up for ever!' (p. 184). Early Americans also claimed to have severed their connection to the past, but Nathaniel Hawthorne insists that in real terms such severance is unattainable.

The tenderness manifested by Pearl following restoration of the stigma to Pearl's breast is the fellow-feeling of the Fallen. Hester must recognise that the child's apparently perverse decision to kiss the scarlet letter is in fact a necessary acknowledgement of the innate sinfulness of all human beings that is implied by the Fall.

Pearl's rejection of the minister is based in this same perception of the need for open acknowledgement of flawed human nature.

It is the adults who now appear perverse, in their fixed determination to depart for a place where they can commence a new life. Nathaniel Hawthorne's concluding description of the landscape, of 'dark, old trees, which, with their multitudinous tongues, would whisper long of what had passed there' suggests the intractability of the real world, and runs emphatically counter to the couple's temporary optimism (p. 186).

CHAPTER 20: THE MINISTER IN A MAZE

> **Dimmesdale returns to the town. His mind becomes focused upon delivery of the Election Sermon on the following day. He appears revitalised, but his moral character has evidently been further damaged. Back in his study, he is visited by Chillingworth. After his departure, Dimmesdale destroys the speech he had prepared and works through the night to produce another**

After glancing back at Hester and Pearl, Dimmesdale returns to the town, his mind filled with the implications of their projected flight to Europe. He is keen to depart on the fourth day from the present, the day following his delivery of the Election Sermon, marking the inauguration of a new Governor. The minister takes pride in sustaining his public face, executing efficiently his professional duties, even as his private face has assumed a dramatically new aspect, based upon his planned flight from the community.

Just as Hester has changed in her outlook and appearance, so the minister has taken on new life, and he approaches the town with unaccustomed vigour. But his moral sense has been compromised in the forest, and he is tempted to sow evil in the world, through such acts as teaching 'wicked words' to small children (p. 192). At a critical point, (according to rumour) a conversation takes place with Mistress Hibbins, the reputed witch. She taunts him with the real import of his visit to the forest: an assignation with the arch-fiend.

Back in his study, Dimmesdale is still haunted by a sense of strangeness, even in so familiar an environment. Roger Chillingworth's arrival in his room appears to him the incarnation of evil. They engage in a conversation charged with irony, and hidden meaning. Left alone, Dimmesdale gives in to his ravenous appetite for food, a concession to bodily pleasure which he has long denied himself. He is driven by impulse to destroy his scholarly preparations for the Election Sermon, and writes another, in an ecstatic state. By next morning, the sermon has been completed.

The portrayal of significant landscape continues at the commencement of this chapter, with a moss-covered tree-trunk, long fallen to the ground. Its weight leaves a grave imprint upon the animate world. Dimmesdale, glancing back, sees Hester and Pearl beside this tell-tale tree-trunk.

The minister is convinced by this glance that he has not just experienced a peculiarly vivid dream. His mind then ranges across his and Hester's plans for the future. Their projections have been made in the wilderness, but the future they intend requires the secure anonymity of Europe's crowded cities. The **pastoral** dream of the New World is here turned on its head.

Discussing the minister's determination to depart after delivery of the prestigious Election Sermon, the narrator teasingly remarks that he hesitates to disclose the minister's motives for this time-scheme; then he proceeds to do so. He is committed 'to hold nothing back from the reader' (p. 188). The thematic concern with disclosure and concealment is in this way incorporated into the actual narration of the story (see Themes). At such moments, Nathaniel Hawthorne keeps his narrator in view as the wry figure we have earlier encountered in 'The Custom-House'.

Returning to Boston, Dimmesdale's perception of the world around him is marked by an 'importunately obtrusive sense of change' (p. 189). Nathaniel Hawthorne stresses the changes wrought in the world by modification of the observer's point of view. Remember that Dimmesdale is a member of that Puritan elite which interprets the world for the townsfolk, acting as privileged readers of God's intention. If his perception is susceptible to such dramatic alteration, what credence should we give to the magistrates' acts of judgemental interpretation? Nathaniel Hawthorne's view was that God had absolute understanding; human beings needed to recognise their own fallibility, and adapt their attitudes accordingly.

The minister has undergone 'a revolution in the sphere of thought and feeling' (pp. 189–90). Note the use of the word 'revolution'. Remember that Nathaniel Hawthorne was living in a society which had assumed its modern aspect following a political revolution only three-quarters of a century before. Additionally, *The Scarlet Letter* is set contemporaneously with the Puritan revolution which led to the overthrow of England's King Charles I, and his supersession by the Lord Protector, Oliver Cromwell.

Dimmesdale belongs to the Puritan establishment, yet he has undergone a rebellion of his emotional being: 'In truth, nothing short of a total change of dynasty and moral code, in that interior kingdom, was adequate to account for the impulses now communicated to the unfortunate and startled minister' (p. 190). The **irony** is that the revolutionary act envisaged by this New England settler is a journey to the security of the Old World.

The narrator makes it clear that the minister has been overtaken by impulses cultivated in the wilderness. In a social context they appear distinctly perverse, and involve a range of gestures calculated to provoke. Dimmesdale struggles to contain this perversity within his customary demeanour of respectability, as he encounters various members of the community upon his return from the forest.

We are seeing the minister in a **metaphorical** maze, trapped by delusory lures and prey to base temptations. Following the preceding scene in which hope of new freedom was attained, here we see Dimmesdale fearing that he is mad, or possessed by the Devil. He has stepped outside of conventional restraints and has discovered that the wild terrain he has entered holds terrible dangers, as well as the promise of joy. Nathaniel Hawthorne felt that this was a lesson from which the Transcendentalists could benefit (see Literary Background).

Despite words of mutual friendship, Dimmesdale and Chillingworth, meeting in the minister's apartment, are both aware that they are in the presence of an enemy. They both have a refined capacity to read with irony. The narrator makes sardonic comment concerning the capacity of words and behaviour to conceal actual feelings and attitudes: 'It is singular however, how long a time often passes before words embody things; and with what security two persons, who choose to avoid a certain subject, may approach its very verge, and retire without disturbing it' (p. 195). The pair talk of medicines and improved health, rather than of the poison that infuses Dimmesdale's moral being and corrupts it utterly.

the Election Sermon a new governor was elected annually in Massachusetts

Ann Turner Ann Turner ran a brothel, and was involved in the murder of Sir Thomas Overbury, in 1613, in the Tower of London. The jailer, Richard Weston, was formerly her servant, and through him poison was administered. She was found guilty of the crime and was hanged in 1615. Turner is relevant because Nathaniel Hawthorne describes Dimmesdale's corruption in terms of the progress of poison through his moral system

CHAPTER 21 : THE NEW ENGLAND HOLIDAY

> The day of the new Governor's inauguration. A crowd has gathered in the market-place to mark the festivities. Hester speaks with a mariner, who confirms that arrangements have been made for the journey to Europe, but adds that Roger Chillingworth will be travelling with them

On the day of the Governor's inauguration, Hester and Pearl arrive in the crowded market-place. The child's conversation again turns to the minister, and Hester asserts that he will not acknowledge them on this day, in this public place.

The Indians, and mariners returned from the Spanish Main, who are present in the market-place, are described as incarnations of wildness. The captain's dress is remarked as signifying his daring character. He confirms to Hester her arrangements for the voyage to England. But he also alarms her by mention that Roger Chillingworth has arranged to make the same crossing. Across the market-place, she perceives the physician smiling with 'secret and fearful meaning' (p. 204).

The crowd in the market-place includes figures dressed in deer-skins, which identifies them as members of forest settlements, rather than citizens of Boston itself. This detail does not merely add historical colour; it augments the book's concern with the way we read codes of dress. Immediately, the narrator turns his attention to the fact that Hester wears her habitual coarse grey garments, even on a public holiday, the only adornment being the scarlet letter.

This concern continues with description of the brightly adorned Pearl: 'The dress, so proper was it to little Pearl, seemed an effluence, or inevitable development and outward manifestation of her character, no more to be separated from her than the many-hued brilliancy from a butterfly's wing, or the painted glory from the leaf of a bright flower. As with these, so with the child; her garb was all of one idea with her nature' (p. 198). Note how naturalness here appears as a positive aspect of Pearl's character. In the broader view, we know that the natural world has a wildness antipathetic to the conduct of a mature and responsible social group.

Nathaniel Hawthorne draws a telling analogy between the festival day in the midst of the Puritan calendar, and the scarlet letter on Hester's drab gown. Hester becomes a 'type' for the body politic. The public officials bear the same kinds of ornate insignia as their Old World equivalents, but the popular entertainments are more muted than the fairs of Elizabethan or Jacobean England.

Amongst those trappings omitted from the New England version are the 'minstrel with his harp and legendary ballad', which should remind us of Nathaniel Hawthorne's comments in 'The Custom-House', that his Puritan ancestors would strongly disapprove of his being a writer. The exclusion of minstrelsy, he observes, is effected 'not only by the rigid discipline of law, but by the general sentiment which gives law its vitality' (p. 201). There is an archness in the narrator's observation that the legacy of puritanism remains strong in New England: 'We have yet to learn again the forgotten art of gayety' (p. 202). Nathaniel Hawthorne appears to be suggesting that as an American writer he suffers general neglect.

Hester notes that the Governor's installation is perceived by citizens to be the commencement of a new and better phase of history: 'For, to-day, a new man is beginning to rule over them; and so – as has been the custom of mankind ever since a nation was first gathered – they make merry and rejoice; as if a good and golden year were at length to pass over the poor old world!' (p. 200). This may be read as further **ironic** comment on the difficulties confronting American aspirations to herald a new epoch of human history. The desire for a new start has a venerable history, and that is, in itself, a telling fact.

Puritan toleration of the ribald ways of the mariners is comparable to Governor Bellingham's taste for beer. It is an indication of occasional flexibility, which compromises the absolutes this community appears to endorse. Many of the citizens 'had not been born to an inheritance of Puritanic gloom', but rather had known families which enjoyed 'the sunny richness of the Elizabethan epoch' (p. 200).

Merry Andrew an habitual colleague of the quack medicine seller, who participated in a dialogue to persuade members of the public to buy their wares

Wrestling-matches, in the differing fashions of Cornwall and Devonshire the rules for wrestling which prevailed in Devon allowed combatants to wear heavy shoes for the purpose of kicking shins

CHAPTER 22: THE PROCESSION

The inaugural procession arrives in the market-place. Dimmesdale, who is notably more energetic than of late, delivers the Election Sermon. Pearl is charged by one of the mariners to convey a message that Chillingworth has undertaken to supervise the minister during his passage to Europe

Hester's alarm at the sight of Chillingworth is compounded by the arrival of the inaugural procession, heralded by the sound of military music.

Dimmesdale's participation in the parade is uncharacteristically forthright.

The sinister Mistress Hibbins seizes the opportunity to pass comment on the minister's changed appearance in a brief conversation with Hester. Hester, standing by that scaffold which had been the scene of her shame, then listens intently to the minister, delivering his sermon. The power of his voice is noted, but also the note of guilt or sorrow which underlay it all, speaking from his heart 'to the great heart of mankind' (p. 211).

Pearl, meanwhile, plays with the Indians and the mariners, who recognise her as a wilder spirit than they. She is charged, by the captain, to deliver a message to her mother, that Chillingworth has given assurance he will take care of arrangements for the minister's journey, and will accompany him. The news devastates the last vestiges of Hester's hopes for freedom.

To heighten her misery, a crowd of people from the neighbouring countryside has assembled to view at first-hand the legendary wearer of the scarlet letter. The mariners and the Indians add their gaze. Finally, the townsfolk join in, regarding the familiar spectacle of the stigma. As she stands within 'that magic circle of ignominy', the minister holds the attention of a worshipful congregation nearby (p. 214).

The latest in a long line of **similes** comparing Pearl to animals, aptly proclaims her to be 'like a bird on the point of taking flight'. But Hester is now conscious that the ways of nature are inappropriate. Her remark, 'We must not always talk in the market-place of what happens to us in the forest', brings together the symbolic arrangement of landscape in the **romance** with the thematic concern for disclosure and concealment in relation to moral standards (p. 208) (see Themes).

Note the significance here of the mariners and the Indians, who feel kinship for Pearl, but who are excluded from recognised social relations. The seamen live a wild life upon the turbulent sea, while the native Americans struggle to survive in the wilderness.

College of Arms the original College was formed in England in 1460/1483. It was responsible for keeping records of those entitled to armorial bearings. Nathaniel Hawthorne misleadingly, and surely ironically given the book's awareness of heraldry (evident in its concluding lines), uses it to suggest a military establishment

Knights Templars an order of the Crusaders founded in 1118, initially to accompany pilgrims to Jerusalem

Bradstreet Simon Bradstreet (1603–97) arrived in New England in 1630, and became a prominent member of Massachusetts society. He was twice Governor

Endicott John Endicott (*c.*1589–1665) was an eminent and rigorously pious figure. He is central to the story 'Endicott and the Red Cross' (1837) (see Nathaniel Hawthorne's Other Works).

Dudley Thomas Dudley (1576–1653) arrived in Massachusetts in 1630 and was elected Governor on four occasions. He was implacably opposed to the spread of democratic government in the colony

Increase Mather Increase Mather (1639–1723) was one of the most esteemed of New England ministers. His scholarship was acknowledged when, in 1685, he was made President of Harvard College, a position he held until 1701

CHAPTER 23: THE REVELATION OF THE SCARLET LETTER

Dimmesdale's inspired address is enthusiastically received. The minister summons Hester and Pearl to join him on the platform. He acknowledges his guilt, and displays the scarlet letter inscribed upon his own breast. Chillingworth declares that Dimmesdale has escaped him. The minister dies

The Election Sermon is over, and Dimmesdale's congregation leaves the church and enters the market-place. All are full of praise for the inspired performance they have witnessed. The minister has spoken of the relationship existing between God and human communities, especially those of New England.

The narrator makes it clear that the minister has attained a moment of glory amongst his fellow citizens rare in this society. In contrast to this, his physical appearance is deathlike. He approaches the scaffold and summons Hester and Pearl to join him there. Frantically, Chillingworth attempts to prevent this reunion. Amidst tumult and confusion, mother and child mount the scaffold and join Dimmesdale.

At last, the minister manages to admit his guilty secret and to make public acknowledgement that Pearl is his child also. In a symbolic revelatory gesture he discloses the scarlet 'A' formed on his own breast by scarification. As he does so, Chillingworth cries out that the minister has escaped him. It is only on this scaffold that the minister could possibly escape the physician's clutches.

Dimmesdale kisses his child, and then he dies, his terrible burden removed. This is 'the great scene of grief' required to develop Pearl's sympathies and to connect her to shared human feelings. Her tears, falling upon her father's cheek, are 'the pledge that she would grow up amid human joy and sorrow, nor for ever do battle with the world, but be a woman in it' (p. 222).

Hester seeks confirmation that the lovers will be united in the afterlife, but Dimmesdale is unwilling to make any such assumption, only to affirm the wisdom and justice of God, and to advise her to entrust her life to Him. Then he leaves this life.

The four main characters are brought together for this dramatic culmination to the story.

With pungent **irony**, the narrator remarks that the minister's speech seemed to certain of his auditors to be like hearing an angel – the signification of the letter 'A' is thrust once more to the foreground of our concerns as we read.

CONCLUSION   **Within a year Chillingworth also died, leaving a considerable inheritance to Hester's daughter. Pearl grew up to become a woman of substance, in England. Hester returned to live in her cottage by the sea, and voluntarily wore the scarlet letter upon her breast**

The narrator comments upon different accounts of the scene, that followed the events of the preceding chapter.

We learn that Chillingworth died within a year, and bequeathed a considerable amount of property, in the Old World and the New, to Pearl. After Chillingworth's demise the mother and child disappear from public view. Various reports concerning them are received, but no concrete evidence. The scarlet letter grows in legend.

One day, Hester arrives at her cottage by the sea. Pearl is not with her, but Hester is known to receive letters and gifts from a loved-one living overseas. It appears that Pearl, the wild elfin child has married into Old World affluence, and has herself become a mother. She does not neglect her own distant and isolated mother.

In later years, of her own free will, Hester assumes the scarlet letter as a symbol upon her bosom. She becomes a counsellor and comforter to troubled members of the community. At her death she is buried near to Dimmesdale. Their dust is kept apart, but they share a tombstone. It bears a simple heraldic device: a red letter A upon a black background.

> The narrator notes that following these events there arose contesting accounts. The narrator advises, 'The reader may choose among these theories' (p. 223). This returns to the book's insistence that facts never exist outside of some interpretative framework. There is always a point of view, explicit or implied, conditioning the way we read events or understand characters.

> In fact, we have been carefully directed by the way the story has been told to reach quite closely delimited conclusions concerning its significance; but it is thematically relevant for the narrator to concede authority to point of view. Apparent facts, such as the letter upon the minister's breast, are denied by certain witnesses. Some onlookers took the minister's embrace of a sinful woman to be enactment of a **parable**, rather than an admission of specific guilt.

> Still the general understanding of his message was that 'we are sinners all alike' (p. 224), and that, for Nathaniel Hawthorne was a salutary lesson. If there is a broad consensual agreement as to meaning, then local variations and discrepancies should encourage a healthy toleration for other views. The record of our collective past is built upon contrary and often conflicting testimonies, yet Nathaniel Hawthorne is insistent that we neglect the legacy of that past to our cost.

> The narrator reminds us that our encounter with the central characters in this story has depended upon discovery of an old

manuscript detailing events. This returns our attention to the historical dimension of the narration. Nathaniel Hawthorne was inviting consideration of changes in the moral climate of New England between the mid seventeenth century and his own day.

The tale may have reached us by an indirect route, but the narrator feels able to make a moral distillation of its message 'Be true! Be true! Be true!' (p. 224). Nathaniel Hawthorne uses the narration to insist that acknowledgement of our frailties is a prerequisite for moral tolerance and social compassion. The Transcendentalists, whom he encountered regularly in Massachusetts, denied innate sinfulness and this meant for him that their moral anchor was discarded (see Literary Background).

We learn that Chillingworth immediately lost all his remaining vitality, 'like an uprooted weed that lies wilting in the sun' (pp. 224–5). This is, of course, another instance of comparison between human beings and plants, which we may interpret in the light Crèvecoeur's famous image (see Literary Background). The physician's life-blood had been concentrated into an act of revenge. Like a parasite deprived of its host, he withers away.

The narrator is moved to make a philosophical observation that love and hatred seem at base to be the same emotion, in that both presuppose an intense focus upon another being. The difference is summed up in that 'one happens to be seen in a celestial radiance, and the other in a dusky and lurid glow' (p. 225). Love is clearly preferable to hatred, but in the fate of Hester and the minister we have seen that love can itself have dire consequences. It is important, in Nathaniel Hawthorne's view to retain a moral perspective that occupies the middle ground between the two extremes.

The narrator speculates that, 'In the spiritual world, the old physician and the minister – mutual victims as they have been – may, unawares, have found their earthly stock of hatred and antipathy transmuted into golden love' (p. 225). The image is suitably alchemical, referring to Chillingworth's past experiments. More importantly, just as no alchemist has managed to find the secret formula transforming base metal into gold, so the reconciliation of these enemies must be entrusted to the operation of God's grace, in a life beyond the earthly grave. Again, Nathaniel Hawthorne saw human limitations as a fact of existence which Emerson and his influential circle needed to recognise (see Literary Background).

Chillingworth's legacy to Pearl continues the theme of inheritance, including the sense that America's history, while separate in certain of its developments, is in many ways inextricably linked to the history of Europe (see Themes). Of equal significance is that Pearl, as an heiress, an inheritor of historical fact, is fully socialised. The wild child is at last accommodated within the laws and customs regulating a human society.

Note that, unlike her mother, Pearl seems to have married most appropriately. Her baby is conceived and born within the law. The chain of human life is extended with this birth, but of equal importance is the link of tender care preserved by Pearl with her mother, despite the distance that separates them. The link cannot be seen, but for Nathaniel Hawthorne it exemplified the most valuable of human resources.

Hester resumes wearing the scarlet letter, and does so as an act of choice. It is likely that she is marking her own flawed character as a way of forming a bridge with other members of the community who need help in their troubled lives. Importantly, the sign takes on differing significance, in this different context; it offers itself to far more benign interpretation, and comes to signify positive qualities. The **polysemous** potential of the sign is now able to be realised.

Hester's belief is that 'a new truth would be revealed, in order to establish the whole relation between man and woman on a surer ground of mutual happiness' (p. 227). Nathaniel Hawthorne would surely have endorsed the view that a finer harmony between male and female values was required in order to create a more compassionate and understanding society.

It seems less likely that he would have subscribed without **irony** to Hester's belief that, 'The angel and apostle of the coming revelation must be a woman, indeed, but lofty, pure, and beautiful; and wise, moreover, not through dusky grief, but the ethereal medium of joy; and showing how sacred love should make us happy, by the truest test of a life successful to such an end!' (p. 228). The vision seems too close to the loftier rhetoric of Margaret Fuller, whom Nathaniel Hawthorne one described as a 'humbug'. But the need for a positive counterbalance to the Puritan emphasis on 'dusky grief' was certainly essential to his view of the requirements for an effective democratic culture.

After the talk of angels and apostles, our focus falls finally upon the letter 'A' carved upon the gravestone erected over the bodies of Hester and Dimmesdale. The sign is now contained within a heraldic device, harking back to the Old World and its long familial lines. The angels and apostles must be accommodated within our recognition of the reality of the passing of historical time, and the fact of our mortality. In the story of Hester Prynne, the capacity of human beings to lead a dignified life despite our flawed nature finds memorable testimony.

Gules   red, in heraldic terms.

PART THREE

CRITICAL APPROACHES

CHARACTERISATION

THE AUTHOR/NARRATOR

Into his tale of the scarlet letter, Nathaniel Hawthorne introduces verifiable historical figures, and grants the authority of a factual account to his work of imaginative fiction. But the boldest gesture of this kind is his inclusion of himself as the narrator of 'The Custom-House'.

The work begins as autobiography, establishing a grounding in personal experience, which forms an accessible bridge for readers to cross into the more remote world of seventeenth-century Boston. Developing his narratorial **persona,** Nathaniel Hawthorne presents himself as editor and elaborator, rather than originator of the story of Hester Prynne. We are lead to feel that we are sharing in his discovery and his efforts to interpret accurately the events and the characters involved.

As editor, Nathaniel Hawthorne becomes far less visible as a character, but the colloquial, conversational voice he establishes in the long introductory section creates a lasting impression of one human being addressing others, without pretension and in the spirit of friendship. The humour of 'The Custom-House' provides necessary leavening for the sombre account which follows.

In contrast with that lively voice, the characters we encounter in 'The Scarlet Letter' itself seem rather like stock figures from an old morality play. The fact that they inhabit a highly stylised landscape, akin to that found in old **allegorical** works, heightens that impression. But if the characters do tend to appear as **symbols,** the narrator's commentary has the effect of disclosing the inadequacy of that kind of understanding. We are encouraged to discover real human intelligence and passion beyond the representation of types.

HESTER PRYNNE

Hester is the embodiment of a passionate and sensual nature. A key to her character is contained in the observation that, 'She had in her nature a rich, voluptuous, Oriental characteristic, – a taste for the gorgeously beautiful' (p. 75). Puritanism disdained pleasures attained through the senses, so Hester's taste, her skills as a needlewoman, and her own appearance, place her beyond the acceptable bounds of Puritan living. Furthermore, she has acted on impulse in entering a love-affair with Dimmesdale, and is clearly guilty when adjudged by Boston's moral laws.

But she is also a victim of an inappropriate marriage to a much older man, and of the circumstances which left her, a young English woman, alone in the New World, while her husband lingered in Europe. Characterisation necessarily focuses upon how she copes with the punishment she endures, and we witness her resourcefulness in containing her impulsive and emotional being within the twin channels of art and altruism. If her social detachment isolates her still further from Puritan norms, her compassion and creativity constitute a substantial step towards a more enlightened conception of social relationships.

Mistress Hibbins tries to persuade Hester to join the company of local witches, but she declines. Witchcraft belongs to the world-view of Puritanism; it was its inverse image, as Nathaniel Hawthorne indicates by having Hibbins share a house with her brother, Governor Bellingham. If Nathaniel Hawthorne's Puritan ancestors had not taken witches seriously they would have felt no need to persecute them. Hester is renouncing the Puritan ethos, and that necessarily includes a refusal to acknowledge witchcraft.

Hester's rebelliousness is of a distinctly more modern kind. The suggestion within *The Scarlet Letter* is that she resembles Anne Hutchinson, that strong woman who spoke out against Puritan orthodoxy, and was driven into exile as a consequence, but Nathaniel Hawthorne undoubtedly had contemporary feminist radicals, such as Margaret Fuller, in mind when he was developing her character. By the end of the novel, Hester has grown from being merely an impulsive adulteress, and has become an introspective visionary, with a revolutionary conception of possible social relationships between men and women.

Nathaniel Hawthorne regarded such political radicalism with disapproval, although he accepted the necessity for reform of those stern codes of conduct governing seventeenth-century New England. It was crucial to his sense of liberal reform that Hester acted with compassion towards fellow Bostonians, displaying much needed tenderness. It was still more important to him that she was accomplished in the art of embroidery, for Nathaniel Hawthorne held that art occupied a pivotal position balancing the interests of head and heart. In his view, it was as an artist, not as an activist, that Hester provided a lesson for the future. Recent feminist criticism has explored the importance of needlecraft as an expressive resource for women lacking a distinctive voice in society. It has also cast a sceptical eye upon the patriarchal assumption that women are inherently suited to be 'angels of mercy' to the community, as an extension of the perceived virtues of wife and mother (see Contemporary Approaches: Feminism).

PEARL

Pearl is seen as a 'little elf', denizen of the world of romance, rather than a socially oriented individual of the kind encountered in realist novels. The child's laughter and tears are extreme responses to situations, signalling a lack of proportion which makes social intercourse and reciprocity difficult.

Like her mother, Pearl lives in isolation, even though she acquires early the ability to speak. The situation is exacerbated by inherited passion, and the fact that the mother and child are persecuted by 'the most intolerant brood that ever lived' (p. 84).

As an energetic sprite, Pearl has considerable charm, but she must move from the animal world into a social context if she is to transform her intuitive moral sense into the responsible conduct of a mature human being. Ultimately, she makes this transition, after sharing in her parents' grief, and comprehending that she too is a Fallen mortal.

Notably, she returns to the Old World in order to grow up. It is possible to read the wayward child as a **personification** of early American lawlessness, of the wild West. The voyage to Europe then becomes an image of America coming to terms with its existence within history, rather than as a manifestation of some eternal mythic newness, unanswerable to any sense of the past.

More immediately, we are able to see Pearl as an incarnation of physical pleasure and imaginative freedom, entirely contrary to the Puritan way of life. Her vitality and attractiveness serve to highlight the limitations of that way of life, although her unruliness also indicates the dangers of uncontrolled indulgence. She is, after all, the living embodiment of that illicit passion which led to the imposition of the scarlet 'A'. Significantly, her mother sustains her love for Pearl, and that declares Hester's refusal to acknowledge her own sinfulness in a way that would make her truly a part of the Puritan system.

ARTHUR DIMMESDALE

Some readers may feel that it is not easy to comprehend the nature of the minister's attraction for Hester Prynne. We are told of his strong animal nature, and of his capacity to hold a congregation enthralled by his charismatic delivery of a sermon. We are also assured that he is generally regarded as a paragon of Christian virtue. But when we actually see Dimmesdale, he is invariably anguished and ailing, immersed in unremitting melancholy, or lacerating his own body.

He is not an attractive figure; but, then, he is an embodiment of the consequences of concealed guilt. Like a haunted character in a **melodrama**, he obsessively raises his hand to his tormented breast. Moreover, he is obsessively proud of his status in the community, and seeks to preserve Boston's high opinion of him at all costs. There is apparent perversity in the way he turns his faith in God as the ultimate judge to ends that seem self-serving, enabling him to sustain his duplicitous facade.

But if Hester is a victim, so is he: pursued relentlessly by the diabolic Chillingworth, and ensnared by the iron framework of the Puritan ethos in which he has been steeped. Still, we can see him as a sympathetic character only in relation to Hester's devotion, the fact that she loves him, and that Pearl intuitively knows him as her father. His final revelation is the grand, but desperate, gesture of an exhausted and morally depleted man.

ROGER CHILLINGWORTH

Chillingworth often appears in the guise of a devil rather than a credible human being, and that is largely a reflection of the way he is perceived by Hester, Dimmesdale and Pearl. Nathaniel Hawthorne puns on the word 'leech', an old term for doctor, in depicting the physician as a parasite sapping the vital energies of the minister, who has committed adultery with his wife.

Like the minister, he lives under concealment, even assuming a false name to protect his identity. He, however, does not put his faith in God. Rather, he assumes divine privilege, prying into the secrets of another man's soul, and violating the sanctity of Dimmesdale's heart. As a godless practitioner of early modern science he seeks power through knowledge. But when he loses his host, his parasitical existence soon comes to an end.

Although he is basically a grotesque and diabolic **caricature**, Chillingworth does have the self-awareness to understand and to concede that his marriage to a young and attractive woman was ill-judged, and has had disastrous consequences. This insight does not, however, result in any act of compassion; rather, it seems to intensify his taste for vengeance. Pearl, the aesthetic creature, needs to be touched by sorrow in order to become a socially responsive human being; Chillingworth, the analytical being, has entirely moved beyond responsive human relationships, and in place of living people he sees only flaws and failings.

THEMES

INHERITANCE

At the end of the story, Pearl benefits from a substantial inheritance left by Chillingworth. If that resolution redeems the physician for us, somewhat, it certainly provides the means for Pearl at last to enter the social world.

But the book's concern with inheritance touches on far larger matters. Nathaniel Hawthorne was concerned that the American emphasis on newness led to irresponsible neglect of continuities with the past, a sense that the new republic stood somehow outside of human history. Ralph Waldo Emerson, America's foremost philosopher at that time, asserted repeatedly that he aspired to live without any sense of the past at his back. Nathaniel Hawthorne recognised this as a dangerous delusion. He believed that unless America saw clearly what it had inherited from the European past, its own potential for improvement would be jeopardised, and the opportunities offered by the democratic system of government would be lost.

A still more fundamental concern for Nathaniel Hawthorne was the Christian belief in Original Sin, which left its trace in all human beings, irrespective of their ostensible differences. The transgression in Eden brought a legacy of work, sin and death into the world. Emerson and his Transcendentalist followers denied that doctrine, and argued that human beings should strive towards perfection in their earthly lives. Whatever the theological argument might be, Nathaniel Hawthorne saw that denial of our shared inheritance of fallibility and mortality could lead in practice to selfishness and insensitivity to the sufferings of others. Acknowledgement of that common legacy was for him the first step towards a tolerant and compassionate understanding of fellow human beings.

HISTORICAL CHANGE

The structure of *The Scarlet Letter* registers historical change as we move back from Massachusetts in the nineteenth century to Massachusetts in the seventeenth century. The awareness of differences in social manners and regulations which this creates is obviously linked closely to the theme of inheritance. Nathaniel Hawthorne was keen to justify the American system of democracy as a real advance in terms of social fairness and toleration, although he was alert to the danger that such gains might be reversed if the lessons of the past were not heeded.

The book identifies a historical trend towards greater liberality, and that is broadly identified with the softening of social attitudes. Nathaniel Hawthorne couches this in terms of gender, suggesting that the conventionally masculine attributes which dominated Puritan Boston have been displaced by more conventionally feminine qualities, including compassion, sensitivity and aesthetic awareness. There is room, however, for further development, and although Nathaniel Hawthorne evidently does not endorse without qualification the feminist position adopted by Hester in the concluding pages, he would have been sympathetic to its broad goals for amelioration of social life (see Contemporary Approaches).

THE SOCIAL FUNCTION OF ART

As Larzer Ziff points out, in *Literary Democracy: the Declaration of Cultural Independence in America* (New York, Viking, 1981), a great deal of early writing in America had a distinctly practical character. Much that was published took the form of journals, sermons, letters, lectures and travelogues. At the time Nathaniel Hawthorne wrote, the status of literary art in America was by no means defined.

Americans were acutely aware that in Europe for centuries literature had been largely reliant on the patronage of the aristocracy. In their modern democracy, there was no such means of financial subsidy, and it is not incidental that *The Scarlet Letter* is prefaced by the author's account of his employment in a Custom-House.

Hester Prynne's artistry in needlework makes a case for the social necessity of art. The stigma is transformed by her skill; it is opened up to multiple meanings, and is consequently enriched. Art, for Nathaniel Hawthorne, had the capacity to mediate between the head and the heart. It channelled passion into forms created through disciplined action, and so avoided the damaging excesses of arid intellect and unruly heart.

In 'The Custom-House', Nathaniel Hawthorne refers to the critical detachment he required for writing. Hester's detachment is a wretched isolation, but nonetheless she worked to serve the community, and for Nathaniel Hawthorne also art was not personal indulgence but a contribution to collective good.

INDIVIDUAL AND COMMUNITY

It is important to remember that the United States, as a modern democratic republic, had been in existence for less than seventy-five years when *The Scarlet Letter* was published in 1850. The nation was heralded as a bold new political experiment, and in Nathaniel Hawthorne's work, as in that of his friend Herman Melville, we can see sustained investigation into the nature of social groups, and of possible relationships between communities and their members. Nathaniel Hawthorne raises issues of rights and obligations, and shows the result of an imbalance in the terms of those agreements that bind members of a society together.

America has always laid emphasis upon the sanctity of the individual as the measure of right and wrong. (The narrator's outrage at Chillingworth's violation of Dimmesdale's soul may be read partly in that light.) There has been distrust especially of government interference in the lives of individual members of American society. Thomas Jefferson, who drafted the Declaration of Independence, and became President of the United States, suggested that that government is best which governs least. The Transcendentalist, Henry David Thoreau went further, and offered the anarchistic view that that government is best which governs not at all (see Literary Background). But if the individual is sacrosanct, America has also been acutely conscious of its particular mode of collective existence, as the first modern democratic republic.

Another of Nathaniel Hawthorne's contemporaries Walt Whitman called his collected poems, *Leaves of Grass* (1855–92), indicating not only the relationship between individual poems and the collection, but also the relationship between individual Americans and the entity known as America. Note that Whitman followed Crèvecoeur in employing an image of plants to convey the nature of American life.

In *The Scarlet Letter*, Nathaniel Hawthorne traces the emergence in Massachusetts of a more compassionate mode of social regulation. But he emphasises the importance of art as a process of individual creativity that can help to advance social conditions, and he stresses the need to base collective understanding on the shared inheritance of human fallibility.

THE IMPORTANCE OF POINT OF VIEW

By enabling us to see Hester's transgression in terms of Puritan morality, and in the light of later, more liberal understanding, Nathaniel Hawthorne establishes a broad field for his thematic concern with the importance of point of view. No facts in *The Scarlet Letter* are given definitive interpretation. Even the death of Dimmesdale, following the revelation of his guilt, is read by eye-witnesses in a number of different ways according to their particular bias. Signs might be described with great precision, but the way in which they are read depends upon a larger context, according to the knowledge and experience of the reader. The relativity of understanding makes tolerance and compassion moral imperatives for Nathaniel Hawthorne.

EXPOSURE AND CONCEALMENT

Chillingworth lurks behind an assumed name. Dimmesdale conceals his sin, and festering in concealment it eats into his soul. Pearl conceals nothing; her entire being is on display, and the effect is overwhelming; it is too much. Hester is exposed to public view, and the stigma upon her breast makes visible the taint in her nature. But although that exposure is intensely painful, the woman manages to transform the nature of the stigmatic token, and the enriched sign not only discloses her guilt, but also manifests her considerable worth.

Total concealment is destructive; total exposure is not tolerable for long. Nathaniel Hawthorne is again taking the middle way between extremes, and insisting upon the importance of artistry in attaining that median.

LANGUAGE AND STYLE

ANACHRONISTIC DICTION

A major concern for Nathaniel Hawthorne was to signal distinctions between Boston society in the early seventeenth century and life in New England in the mid nineteenth century. The language he employs is a convenient means to suggest wider social differences. 'The Custom-House', which is written in an easy colloquial style, conveys a relaxed democratic voice. It is conversational and addressed to contemporaries.

The story of Hester Prynne is not written in seventeenth-century English style, but it has a stylised period feel, largely resulting from **anachronistic** diction and phrasing, included in the instances of direct speech. For example, at the end of Chapter 6, Hester speaks to her daughter:

> 'Hush, Pearl, hush! Thou must not talk so!' answered the mother, suppressing
> a groan. 'He sent us all into this world. He sent even me, thy mother. Then,

much more, thee! Or, if not, thou strange and elfish child, whence didst thou come?' (p. 88)

Obviously, the antiquated second-person singular forms 'thou', 'thee' and 'thy' identify that Hester is speaking in an earlier century. The concluding phrase would appear in modern form as, 'where did you come from?'. The word 'whence' had become far less familiar by Nathaniel Hawthorne's day, while 'didst' had been universally superseded by plain 'did'.

VERBAL PATTERNING

One of the distinguishing features of literary language is its self-conscious patterning. This is very evident in that kind of poetry which rhymes, creating links between words through audible echoes. But verbal patterning is also a feature of many prose works, and Nathaniel Hawthorne uses a number of key words strategically throughout *The Scarlet Letter*. They recur in various contexts creating connections between apparently disparate characters and events. In this way they help to direct our interpretation, sometimes without us being aware that this is happening.

A prominent example is the word 'impulse'. It signifies motivation for action which is beyond conscious control. In Margaret Fuller's diaries we find that she and her circle devoted time to discussing this word's significance for their understanding of human nature. Nathaniel Hawthorne uses it extensively in his other writings.

Here we are introduced to it in the first sentence of 'The Custom-House', where the narrator refers to 'an autobiographical impulse' which has driven him to write the account. An unlikely link is thus created with Hester Prynne, whose actions are regularly attributed to 'impulse'. But the word is also attached to other characters in the tale. We are told, for example, that it was Dimmesdale's 'genuine impulse to adore the truth' (p. 125).

It was 'impulse' which lead Hester and Dimmesdale to develop their love-affair, despite her being married and him being a minister. Nathaniel Hawthorne viewed impulsiveness as evidence of our vestigial animal nature. Social existence necessitated its regulation through the distinctly human faculty of reason. Art offered a viable means to balance animalistic impulsiveness and human rationality.

READING SIGNS

The journals kept by early Puritan settlers in New England are fascinating examples of compulsive interpretation. All events were read as signs of God's intentions for the newly established communities. Even on the journey across the ocean to the New World, the Puritans were alert to any sign which might reveal God's pleasure or displeasure in their actions. A chicken falling overboard might be seen as a manifestation of some divine meaning.

Once ashore, the environment was so strange to European eyes, that Old World language sat uneasily upon the landscape. Towns were often named after familiar places in England, as if the name tamed the wilderness, and forced it to conform to the settlers' requirements. Boston, Massachusetts took its name from Boston, Lincolnshire.

The Puritans were, then, exceptionally alert to signs, and aware of the power of those verbal signs we call words. Nathaniel Hawthorne takes the first letter of the alphabet as the focal point for his story. The Puritan magistrates had no doubt as to the meaning of that scarlet 'A'. But Nathaniel Hawthorne opens up its meaning, showing that all signs have the capacity to be **polysemous**, to carry multiple meanings.

The narration makes us aware in a number of ways of our own acts of interpretation. We are aware of joining the narrator, and the characters in the tale, in reading signs, and become concerned to make our readings as accurate as possible. At the same time, we are aware that interpretation often produces divergent or conflicting results, according to point of view.

Nathaniel Hawthorne's liberal contention is that we need to draw from such divergence the conclusion that a flexible and tolerant morality is an essential component of any social group. The rigidity of Puritan readings, which claimed divine authority, needs to be modified in accordance with our acknowledgement that we are fallible human beings.

A literary consequence of the concern with reading signs is that at times *The Scarlet Letter* anticipates subsequent developments in detective fiction. It also anticipates the contemporary critical approach known as **semiotics**, which assumes that the world as it exists in our understanding is necessarily a structure of signs (see Contemporary Approaches).

ALLEGORY AND ITS LIMITATIONS

Allegory is a narrative which has a coherent system of meaning behind the obvious, surface sense. Allegorical interpretation takes the characters, events, and landscape of a tale to be symbols which, once deciphered, reveal a more profound structure of significance. One of the best-known examples of allegory is John Bunyan's *The Pilgrim's Progress* (1678), in which the hero's journey across a highly stylised landscape, peopled with purposefully contrived figures, symbolises Christian striving for salvation.

Nathaniel Hawthorne especially admired Edmund Spenser's long poem *The Faerie Queene* (1590, 1596), which is an allegory of the formation of national identity under Queen Elizabeth, as well as an allegory of Christian quest for Truth. Truth is symbolised in Spenser's poem by a woman named Una (the Latin word meaning, 'one'), who rides upon a lion. Nathaniel Hawthorne and his wife named their baby daughter, Una. Lion was the name of the family's cat.

In *The Scarlet Letter*, Nathaniel Hawthorne uses conventions of this venerable mode of writing and reading, in order to show its limitations. The landscape is stylised in a way that compels us to read it in symbolic terms. So the forest stands for moral confusion, and the sea for unbounded human thought, while the town's cemetery and jail represent the innate sinfulness of human beings. The characterisation is also allegorical: for example, Pearl symbolises wild, lawless energy, and Chillingworth stands for the unrestrained intellect, prying beyond what is proper to human knowledge.

The trappings of classic allegory compel us to read in a particular way, looking for a coherent structure of correspondences. But Nathaniel Hawthorne knew that modern readers, accustomed to greater subtlety in characterisation and narration would resist straightforward allegorical reading, and *The Scarlet Letter* uses our sense of the limitations of this mode in order to make a pressing moral point. At times the symbolism is excessively crude, and this contributes to our awareness that life is more complex than allegorical reading can acknowledge.

Starting with the wild rose-bush located beside the prison-door, the symbolism of the tale is systematically overdetermined; that is, it is laden with meaning that is too narrowly fixed. We come to perceive that the relationship of Hester Prynne and Arthur Dimmesdale is inadequately served by such a closely controlled allegorical system. Parallel to this, we come to recognise the inadequacy of the Puritan way of interpreting the world, as a viable moral system. The focus for both systems is the scarlet 'A' carried on the breast of each lover. Nathaniel Hawthorne concertedly opens up this sign to allow multiple meanings, and in the process he undermines both the coherence of allegory, and the authority of Puritan law. In their place he installs a more subtle and expansive mode of reading, and a more tolerant and flexible moral understanding.

THE PARTICIPATING NARRATOR

The Scarlet Letter begins as an autobiographical account. Nathaniel Hawthorne speaks, in the first-person, of his own experiences in the Salem Custom-House. But it is soon evident that this is not simply a documentary account. The details on which he tellingly lingers, the lively and purposeful characterisation of his colleagues, and the commentary he introduces all suggest that we are being addressed not by Nathaniel Hawthorne as such, but by 'Nathaniel Hawthorne', a stylised narrator. The voice is carefully and deliberately crafted to create a certain tone, drawing us into its confidence, and inviting us to share in the discovery of an old manuscript.

The narrator then becomes editor and elaborator of that manuscript. As we start to read the actual tale of 'The Scarlet Letter' we are struck by the difference in tone to the preceding section, 'The Custom-House'. We have entered a far more sombre and formal world. In many ways it will appear alien to us. But the narrative voice, although it has shifted to third-person, has brought us into this world to share in the effort to interpret accurately. Occasionally, his voice addresses us directly, to remind us of the joint venture. He is convinced of the relevance of this story of the past, and encourages us to discern personal relevance in it.

Note that the description, in 'The Custom-House', of the narrator's discovery of the story's raw materials, and of his struggle to find a way of composing them into a tellable tale prepares us for the distinctive structure of *The Scarlet Letter*. There is not a great deal of action in the story; rather it can be seen as a drama of interpretation. There is a sequence of scenes in which events occur, ranging from Hester's interview with the Governor to the appearance of the scarlet letter 'A' as a light in the night sky. These are presumably to be seen as refinements and elaborations of events recorded in the earlier manuscript. They are interspersed with lengthy discussions of character and of motivation, which may be seen as the narrator's attempts to interpret the raw information, in order to grant it a moral dimension, and to establish its relevance for himself and for his readers. For Nathaniel Hawthorne, **romance** was not a flight from the real world, but the means for a more accurate and responsive relationship to it.

ROMANCE

Some of the best-known American works of prose fiction can be classified as **romances**. Amongst Nathaniel Hawthorne's predecessors, we can cite the example of James Fenimore Cooper, in *The Last of the Mohicans* (1826). Amongst later writers, F. Scott Fitzgerald's *The Great Gatsby* (1925) is a noteworthy example. American writers seem to have been especially conscious of an imaginative vision of their country which has always coloured, and at times has shaped, its historical reality. Romance has enabled to render that in literary form.

'The Custom-House' contains a classic description of the nature of romance. Essentially, this mode of writing involves a blending of the Actual and the Imaginary, granting the familiar world an unfamiliar aspect. Far from being a distortion of reality, Nathaniel Hawthorne understood this to be an accurate reflection of the way in which we all rely upon imaginative projection to make sense of the world around us. A practical result of this is that the same event can be read in markedly different ways according to the perceiver's point of view.

The scarlet 'A' is presented as the distillation of romance. It is a familiar letter, with a measurable, material reality, yet through embroidery Hester has transformed it into a sign which is open to a range of interpretations and an enrichment of meaning.

PART FOUR

TEXTUAL ANALYSIS

TEXT 1   (PAGES 35–6)

The same torpor, as regarded the capacity for intellectual effort, accompanied me home, and weighed upon me in the chamber which I most absurdly termed my study. Nor did it quit me, when, late at night, I sat in the deserted parlour, lighted only by the glimmering coal-fire and the moon, striving to picture forth imaginary scenes, which, the next day, might flow out on the brightening page in many-hued description.

If the imaginative faculty refused to act at such an hour, it might well be deemed a hopeless case. Moonlight, in a familiar room, falling so white upon the carpet, and showing all its figures so distinctly, – making every object so minutely visible, yet so unlike a morning or noontide visibility, – is a medium the most suitable for a romance-writer to get acquainted with his illusive guests. There is the little domestic scenery of the well-known apartment; the chairs, with each its separate individuality; the centre-table, sustaining a work-basket, a volume or two, and an extinguished lamp; the sofa; the book-case; the picture on the wall; all these details, so completely seen, are so spiritualized by the unusual light, that they seem to lose their actual substance, and become things of intellect. Nothing is too small or too trifling to undergo this change, and acquire dignity thereby. A child's shoe; the doll, seated in her little wicker carriage; the hobby-horse; – whatever, in a word, has been used or played with, during the day, is now invested with a quality of strangeness and remoteness, though still almost as vividly present as by daylight. Thus, therefore, the floor of our familiar room has become a neutral territory, somewhere between the real world and fairy-land, where the Actual and the Imaginary may meet, and each imbue itself with the nature of the other. Ghosts might enter here, without affrighting us. It would be too much in keeping with the scene to excite surprise, were we to look about us and discover a form, beloved, but gone hence, now sitting quietly in a streak of this magic moonshine, with an aspect that would make us doubt whether it had returned from afar, or had never once stirred from our fireside.

The somewhat dim coal-fire has an essential influence in producing the effect which I would describe. It throws its unobtrusive tinge throughout the room, with a faint ruddiness upon the walls and ceiling, and a reflected gleam from the polish of the furniture. This warmer light mingles itself with the cold spirituality of the moonbeams, and communicates, as it were, a heart and sensibilities of human tenderness to the forms which fancy summons up. It converts them from snow-images into men and women. Glancing at the looking-glass, we behold – deep within its haunted verge – the smouldering glow of the half-extinguished anthracite, the white moonbeams on the floor, and a repetition of all the gleam and shadow of the picture, with one remove farther from the actual, and nearer to the imaginative. Then, at such an hour, and with this scene before him, if a man, sitting all alone, cannot dream strange things, and make them look like truth, he need never try to write romances.

This passage has become famous for its description of the nature of **romance**. The 'torpor' to which the narrator refers is the sluggishness in his creativity that has followed upon employment as a surveyor in the Custom-House. The position enabled him to discover the raw materials for the story that follows, but labour within an institution stemmed the flow of his creative energies.

This places us in the narrator's debt, we become aware of the struggle involved in the composition of this book. But it has a more specific thematic relevance to the tale, 'The Scarlet Letter'. Nathaniel Hawthorne is making a case, which would have been familiar to him from the writings of European **Romanticism**, that the artist is necessarily something of an outsider. In order to gain critical detachment from society, and in order to achieve the personal freedom necessary to enable creativity to flourish, a writer must be set apart from routine and regulation.

Of course, Hester Prynne's artistry flourishes when she is condemned to live on the margins of society. The identification of the narrator with the bearer of the scarlet letter, which began with use of the word 'impulse' in the first sentence, is continued here. Despite their evident differences, both might justifiably wear an 'A' to signify 'artist'. The identification is reinforced in the lines preceding this passage by the fact that escaping his confinement in a government institution, the narrator would go for 'sea-shore walks and rambles in the country'. This is very similar to the terrain Hester Prynne inhabits: released from detention, she is seen walking by the shore or wandering in the forest.

Note that for the Transcendentalists, solitary walking in a natural environment was a means to discover the divinity within oneself (see Literary Background). In Hester's case, on the contrary, it offers occasion for her to meditate upon her own sinfulness.

The narrator refers to 'the chamber which I most absurdly termed my study'. This chamber might be recalled by those scholarly rooms which Dimmesdale and Chillingworth rent. A much more important point here, however, is that the narrator persists in applying the word 'study' to a room which is not used for studying. The slipperiness of the verbal sign lies at the heart of our response to Hester's story. The 'A' remains, but does it still signify 'adulteress', or do changing circumstances alter the meaning of that letter?

The definition of romance begins by establishing the kind of lighting that is required to stimulate the imagination. The glare of sunlight, which we may associate with the power of the mind, or rational control, is notably absent. Rather, we have its subdued and indirect reflection from the moon, and the glow of a coal-fire. Reason alone, applied direct, will not produce art. Some form of imaginative mediation is required.

Note that lighting effects play an important role in *The Scarlet Letter*. We see Pearl dancing like a sprite between sunlight and shadows, eluding the grasp of the reasoning mind; we see Dimmesdale illuminated on the scaffold by an unearthly light in the night sky; and those coals assume the sinister glow of the infernal regions.

It is important to recognise that the romance-writer is not indulging in unconstrained invention; rather, the 'familiar' is an essential element. Romance is a modification of reality, not a flight from it. In a sense, romance can be seen as a more accurate portrayal of our existence in the world than supposedly realistic documentary accounts. In our daily relationships with people, objects, events and places there is always an element of imaginative projection, which allows us to feel that we are not merely in their presence, but have some form of understanding of them. This understanding might not be amenable to any form of scientific proof, but it is vital to our sense of reality.

Note that efforts to understand through imaginative interpretation are encountered regularly throughout *The Scarlet Letter*. These interpretations are often at variance, although the stark facts remain the same. So, in 'The Custom-House' we are told of the discovery of a piece of cloth, which can be measured, according to good scientific principles, but its meaning remains an issue for the imagination to resolve.

The narrator invokes a range of familiar objects by naming them. He then remarks how moonlight invests them with 'a quality of strangeness and remoteness', even though they remain palpably present. It is instructive to compare with this the effect of Hester's needlework upon the scarlet 'A'. We are told in Chapter 2, that onlookers seeing it 'so fantastically embroidered and illuminated upon her bosom', even though they 'had been familiarly acquainted with Hester Prynne, were now impressed as if they beheld her for the first time' (p. 51). It is evident that the letter is itself an embodiment of romance, at once familiar and estranging.

Estrangement, or **defamiliarisation**, is one of the key concepts in Romantic aesthetics. It refers to strategies of writing which make the world appear in an unusual light, and so challenge our familiar sense of it. Famous descriptions of the process, formulated by English poets, are to be found in Coleridge's *Biographia Literaria* (1817), and Shelley's *The Defence of Poetry* (1821; published 1840). In both cases, the intention is to establish for readers a more accurate relationship to reality. That is Nathaniel Hawthorne's intention also, even though he speaks of romance as 'a neutral territory, somewhere between the real world and fairy-land'.

The point, as we have seen, is that 'the Actual and the Imaginary' meet constantly in the way we interpret and come to understand our experiences. In romance, Nathaniel Hawthorne is enabled to bring together Actual historical figures, such as Governor Bellingham and the Reverend Wilson, with such creatures of the Imagination as Pearl and Roger Chillingworth. Language is a medium which allows their co-existence, because in books real human beings and fictional inventions all take form through words.

Remember that 'Nathaniel Hawthorne' identified an author when it appeared on the title-page of a book, but it could also be found stamped on packages passing through the Salem Custom-House. The name in that context looked exactly the same, but it did not carry the same meaning as those words when they appear in an account of literary history.

There are elements in *The Scarlet Letter*, such as the hysterical appearances of Mistress Hibbins, and the diabolic interventions of Chillingworth, which would not be out of place in a **Gothic** horror story. But despite those trappings, the kind of ghost which Nathaniel Hawthorne is more concerned with is 'a form, beloved, but gone hence', apparently occupying a familiar space in a way that does not cause distress, yet prompts us to question the evidence of our senses.

The warmth of human emotion is here figured in the image of the glowing fire, which significantly has a reddish tinge. It is through this emotional element that the apparitions are transformed, from 'snow-images' conjured through the 'magic moonshine' of artistic invention, into living men and women, with passions and sympathies.

Seen in a looking-glass, the room looks still stranger, taken one step further from the familiar. In the mirror, the narrator would be accustomed to see his own image, and in the composition of the tale that follows he has looked into himself and found that it also reveals truths discovered there. It is important for Nathaniel Hawthorne that we read his romance in such a way that we can perceive its moral relevance to us all.

TEXT 2   (PAGES 135–7)

Nothing was more common, in those days, than to interpret all meteoric appearances, and other natural phenomena, that occurred with less regularity than the rise and set of sun and moon, as so many revelations from a supernatural source. Thus, a blazing spear, a sword of flame, a bow, or a sheaf of arrows, seen in the midnight sky, prefigured Indian warfare. Pestilence was known to have been foreboded by a shower of crimson light. We doubt whether any marked event, for good or evil, ever befell New England, from its settlement down to Revolutionary times, of which the inhabitants had not been previously warned by some spectacle of this nature. Not seldom, it had been seen by multitudes. Oftener, however, its credibility rested on the faith of some lonely eyewitness, who beheld the wonder through the colored, magnifying, and distorting medium of his imagination, and shaped it more distinctly in his afterthought. It was, indeed, a majestic idea, that the destiny of nations should be revealed, in these awful hieroglyphics, on the cope of heaven. A scroll so wide might not be deemed too expansive for Providence to write a people's doom upon. The belief was a favorite one with our forefathers, as betokening that their infant commonwealth was under a celestial guardianship of peculiar intimacy and strictness. But what shall we say, when an individual discovers a revelation, addressed to himself alone, on the same vast sheet of record! In such a case, it could only be the symptom of a highly disordered mental state, when a man, rendered morbidly self-contemplative by long, intense, and secret pain, had extended his egotism over the whole expanse of nature, until the firmament itself should appear no more than a fitting page for his soul's history and fate.

We impute it, therefore, solely to the disease in his own eye and heart, that the minister, looking upward to the zenith, beheld there the appearance of an immense letter, – the letter A, – marked out in lines of dull red light. Not but the meteor may have shown itself at that point, burning duskily through a veil of cloud; but with no such shape as his guilty imagination gave it; or, at least, with so little definiteness, that another's guilt might have seen another symbol in it.

There was a singular circumstance that characterized Mr. Dimmesdale's psychological state, at this moment. All the time that he gazed upward to the zenith, he was, nevertheless, perfectly aware that little Pearl was pointing her finger towards old Roger Chillingworth, who stood at no great distance from the scaffold. The minister appeared to see him, with the same glance that discerned the miraculous letter. To his features, as to all other objects, the meteoric light imparted a new expression; or it might well be that the physician was not careful then, as at all other times, to hide the malevolence with which he looked upon his victim. Certainly, if the meteor kindled up the sky, and disclosed the earth, with an awfulness that admonished Hester Prynne and the clergyman of the day of judgment, then might Roger Chillingworth have passed with them for the arch-fiend, standing there, with a smile and scowl, to claim his own. So vivid was the expression, or so intense the minister's perception of it, that it seemed still to remain painted on the darkness, after the meteor had vanished, with an effect as if the street and all things else were at once annihilated.

This passage follows the scene in which a scarlet letter 'A' is seen glowing in the sky. Henry James, in *Hawthorne* (1879) argued that scene was overdone, so that it verged on 'physical comedy'. Nathaniel Hawthorne evidently thought the risk worthwhile as it allowed him to suggest a universal stigma, indicating our common fallibility. It also facilitated the discussion here of the exegetical mentality of the New England Puritans, their habit of reading the world as if it were God's book.

Nathaniel Hawthorne remarks that this community, with its striking combination of self-assurance and nervousness, perceived natural phenomena as divinely ordained symbols. Modern science has rendered meteors comprehensible, although they may still excite wonder, even in sophisticated viewers. It is noticeable, however, that the terms of Puritan interpretation are bound to their immediate daily concerns: fear of Indian attack, and dread of disease. The habit persisted in New England, he asserts, until Revolutionary times. Remember, this was only seventy-four years previously. The suggestion is that America's shift to democracy was a move into modern ways of thinking, and such superstition became inappropriate.

The importance of point of view, and the crucial role played by imagination in our understanding of the world are major themes of the book (see Themes). They are both touched upon here, with reference to the observer who perceived a sign 'through the colored, magnifying, and distorting medium of his imagination'. The imagination is not merely the province of the artist; it is a key component in the process by which we all come to know reality. It may alter the way the facts appear, but that is an essential aspect of human consciousness.

The narrator emphasises that such exegesis was common amongst those who sought to justify the existence of New England as a society set up with God's special approval. The anomaly in this case is that Dimmesdale saw the sign to be directed to him alone. That is symptomatic of his self-obsession, and of the guilt that follows from prolonged concealment of his sin. His obsession shapes his point of view; 'another's guilt may have seen another symbol in it'. Note how the narrator is here conducting his own investigation into how signs generate meaning, a broader field of research than mere reconstruction of past events. Modern Americans may accept scientific explanations, but they are still tied to points of view, formed in relation to their most pressing personal concerns.

Dimmesdale here receives analysis of a kind that anticipates the characterisation favoured by later works of **psychological realism**. But the narrator then directs our attention to Pearl, who is pointing at Chillingworth. These are figures from an **allegory**, rather than realistically developed characters. They are ultimately two-dimensional figures, whereas Dimmesdale is scrutinised in three-dimensional depth. This is the blend facilitated by **romance**, with its fusion of the real world and fairy-land. If historical change is registered in the passage from superstitious to scientific understanding, it is also evident in Nathaniel Hawthorne's bold juxtaposition of an older allegorical mode with a modern psychological approach to interpretation.

TEXT 3   (PAGES 227–8)

In fine, the gossips of that day believed, – and Mr. Surveyor Pue, who made investigations a century later, believed, – and one of his recent successors in office, moreover, faithfully believes, – that Pearl was not only alive, but married, and happy, and mindful of her mother; and that she would most joyfully have entertained that sad and lonely mother at her fireside.

But there was a more real life for Hester Prynne, here, in New England, than in that unknown region where Pearl had found a home. Here had been her sin; here, her sorrow; and here was yet to be her penitence. She had returned, therefore, and resumed, – of her own free will, for not the sternest magistrate of that iron period would have imposed it, – resumed the symbol of which we have related so dark a tale. Never afterwards did it quit her bosom. But, in the lapse of the toilsome, thoughtful, and self-devoted years that made up Hester's life, the scarlet letter ceased to be a stigma which attracted the world's scorn and bitterness, and became a type of something to be sorrowed over, and looked upon with awe, yet with reverence too. And, as Hester Prynne had no selfish ends, nor lived in any measure for her own profit and enjoyment, people brought all their sorrows and perplexities, and besought her counsel, as one who had herself gone through a mighty trouble. Women, more especially, – in the continually recurring trials of wounded, wasted, wronged, misplaced, or erring and sinful passion, – or with the dreary burden of a heart unyielded, because unvalued and unsought, – came to Hester's cottage, demanding why they were so wretched, and what the remedy! Hester comforted and counselled them, as best she might. She assured them, too, of her firm belief, that, at some brighter period, when the world should have grown ripe for it, in Heaven's own time, a new truth would be revealed, in order to establish the whole relation between man and woman on surer ground of mutual happiness. Earlier in life, Hester had vainly imagined that she herself might be the destined prophetess, but had long since recognized the impossibility that any mission of divine and mysterious truth should be confided to a woman stained with sin, bowed down with shame, or even burdened with a life-long sorrow. The angel and apostle of the coming revelation must be a woman, indeed, but lofty, pure, and beautiful; and wise, moreover, not through dusky grief, but the ethereal medium of joy; and showing how sacred love should make us happy, by the truest test of a life successful to such an end!

So said Hester Prynne, and glanced her sad eyes downward at the scarlet letter. And, after many, many years, a new grave was delved, near an old and sunken one, in that burial-ground beside which King's Chapel has since been built. It was near that old and sunken grave, yet with a space between, as if the dust of the two sleepers had no right to mingle. Yet one tombstone served for both. All around, there were monuments carved with armorial bearings; and on this simple slab of slate – as the curious investigator may still discern, and perplex himself with the purport – there appeared the semblance of an engraved escutcheon. It bore a device, a herald's wording of which might serve for a motto and brief description of our now concluded legend; so sombre is it, and relieved only by one ever-glowing point of light gloomier than the shadow:-

"ON A FIELD, SABLE, THE LETTER A. GULES"

In Chapter 2, the word 'gossips' is used in its seventeenth-century sense of 'relative in God', indicating friendship through spiritual affinity. Here it is used, apparently, in its modern sense of 'idle talkers'. In the first instance, it featured in direct speech, and was an instance of anachronistic diction; here it is part of the narrator's commentary (see Language and Style). It conforms to the theme of historical change (see Themes), but more importantly it discloses how the meaning of a sign can change according to context. 'Gossips' is physically the same word, but it is to be read in a different way. The relevance of this to Nathaniel Hawthorne's insistence on the **polysemous** nature of the scarlet 'A' is clear.

If history involves change, it also involves continuity. That is crucial to the book's concern with inheritance (see Themes). There is constancy of interpretation from Hester Prynne's contemporaries, through the compiler of the account, to its later editor, and by implication to us also, as readers, with regard to Pearl's fate.

Note that here, unlike, say, the culminating scene on the scaffold, which had many witnesses yet still generated different versions, there is little supporting evidence concerning Pearl's subsequent history, and yet there is interpretative accord. We may see personal bias in the narrator's willingness to believe that all turned out well, and that Pearl developed into a loving daughter.

She could not credibly have entered into Puritan society after its treatment of her mother. Yet Nathaniel Hawthorne had to have her socialised. So, **ironically**, she returns to the Old World, ensuring her future by connecting with the past. Hester also connects to the past by returning to New England, the site of her transgression. By continuing to acknowledge her own sin, she is accepting the legacy of Original Sin, which Nathaniel Hawthorne saw as the basis for human mutuality.

Assuming the scarlet 'A' of her own free will, Hester may be commemorating Arthur, her lover; or she may be identifying America, as the country to which she now ties her hopes for the future of humankind. And there are numerous other possibilities, since the sign has been released from the rigid control of the Puritan patriarchy.

In his story 'Ethan Brand' (1851), Nathaniel Hawthorne writes of 'the magnetic chain of humanity', signifying the impalpable, yet real bonds that hold human beings together despite their differences. Hester's admission of her sinfulness exercises a kind of magnetic attraction, drawing other troubled people to her door. Her adultery was a serious failing, but she has transformed it into a bridge for other Fallen men and women to cross. By listening with sympathy and sharing the burden of guilt, Hester saved many people from the doom that befell Dimmesdale in his solitary torment.

She is, despite her ordeal, affirmative in her vision of future relationships between men and women. Nathaniel Hawthorne seems to allude to the Transcendentalist Margaret Fuller in his reference to Hester's youthful desire to become a prophetess. That was a guise which Fuller often adopted. Her view of her own mission, expressed notably in *Woman in the Nineteenth Century* (1845), seems to be closely echoed in Hester's belief that a noble woman will one day teach that 'sacred love should make us happy'. But Hester's 'A' stands neither for angel, nor apostle, because she is after all a mere mortal. Fuller too was a woman who, despite her extraordinary capabilities, had failings of which Nathaniel Hawthorne was acutely conscious.

Nathaniel Hawthorne is not espousing Hester's final vision of a 'coming revelation', although he saw the extended influence of women as a vital civilising influence in American life. The vision is succeeded by the reality of human mortality, the inevitable end to an earthly, not an angelic life. Hester is buried in the historical earth.

Her monument carries an heraldic design, which in its form provides a final link to the ancient lineage of Europe. This sign of mortality is, like her personal stigma, enriched by embellishment. Hester and Dimmesdale lie in separate, yet adjacent graves. There is no assurance of their reunion in an afterlife. But there is a union through the single tombstone that signifies their shared sinfulness, and through that sign they are joined to humanity in general. For, as we saw at the start of the tale, the cemetery betokens our common inheritance and our common fate.

PART FIVE

BACKGROUND

BRIEF BIOGRAPHY

Nathaniel Hawthorne was born in Salem, Massachusetts, on Independence Day (July 4th), 1804. He alludes in 'The Custom-House' to his ancestor, Major William Hathorne (1607–81), the first member of the family to arrive in Massachusetts, from England, in 1630. His father, who was a sea-captain, preserved the spelling Hathorne. Nathaniel added the 'w'. His father died in 1808, leaving his wife and children financially dependent upon her family.

In 1821 Nathaniel Hawthorne became a student at Bowdoin College, Brunswick, Maine. On graduating, in 1825, he returned to Salem. In 1836, he moved to Boston, where he worked as a magazine editor. In 1839 he took up a post in the Boston Custom House. He resigned from that at the beginning of 1841, and returned to Salem.

In April 1841, he joined the Brook Farm communitarian experiment. He left after eight months, but his experiences there provided the basis for *The Blithedale Romance* (1852). In 1842, he married Sophia Peabody, and the couple moved to the Old Manse, in Concord, Massachusetts. They had three children: Una, born in 1844; Julian, in 1846; and Rose, in 1851.

Nathaniel Hawthorne struggled to support his family, but in 1846, he was appointed Surveyor at Salem Custom House, where he remained until 1849, when a change in the presidency resulted in loss of office. In 1850, he met the writer Herman Melville, who became one of his closest friends.

In 1853, he travelled to England as American consul, based in Liverpool and Manchester. He journeyed through France and Italy before returning to the United States in 1860. He died in 1864.

A substantial account of Nathaniel Hawthorne's life is given in Arlin Turner's *Nathaniel Hawthorne: A Biography* (Oxford, OUP, 1980). Pertinent details of his ancestry are uncovered by Vernon Loggins in *The Hawthornes: The Story of Seven Generations of an American Family* (New York, Greenwood Press, 1968).

Nathaniel Hawthorne's other works

Nathaniel Hawthorne began to publish stories regularly in the 1830s. Many of them, such as 'Young Goodman Brown' and 'The Maypole of Merry Mount', dealt with the Puritan past. The collection *Twice-Told Tales* which appeared in 1837, included 'Endicott and the Red Cross', a story which has direct bearing on *The Scarlet Letter*. It is also a tale of seventeenth-century New England. More specifically, it includes the figure of a beautiful woman, forced to wear a scarlet 'A' upon her breast. The sign has been embroidered, like the one Hester wears, and the narrator comments that it seemed to mean 'Admirable', or anything other than 'Adulteress'.

Other stories have an evident bearing upon *The Scarlet Letter*. For example, 'The Celestial Railroad' (1843), is a concerted **satire** on Transcendentalist optimism. 'The Birthmark' (1843), tells of a beautiful woman who is considered perfect apart from a deforming birthmark. Her husband surgically removes this blight and the woman dies. The mark was the stigmatic sign of innate imperfection, and her death is proof that to reach perfection on earth is not the fate of human beings. 'Ethan Brand' (1851) is a powerful story of a man driven by an obsessive interest in another human being's inner self; the similarity to Chillingworth's attention to Dimmesdale is self-evident.

Nathaniel Hawthorne's other full-length prose works can all be categorised as **romances.** *The House of Seven Gables* (1851), pursues the theme of human sinfulness through a dramatic story set in nineteenth-century Salem. *The Blithedale Romance* (1852), traces Nathaniel Hawthorne's growing disillusionment with Transcendentalist idealism through a fictionalised account of his life as a member of an experimental commune. *The Marble Faun* (1860), is set in Rome, and as well as continuing Nathaniel Hawthorne's familiar moral concerns, it develops his meditations on the social status of art.

The history of modern America is crucially an extended account of immigration, with waves of newcomers displacing the indigenous population, often through force.

The first permanent colony in New England was established at Plymouth, Massachusetts, in 1620. During the nineteenth century, these pioneering settlers became known as the 'Pilgrim Fathers', highlighting the fact that their precarious voyage across the Atlantic Ocean was essentially a pilgrimage in search of religious freedom.

In 1534, Henry VIII had broken with the religious authority of the Pope. Throughout the sixteenth century, the nature of the relationship between England and Rome fluctuated dramatically. Under Queen Mary, for example, Roman Catholicism was restored, and followers of the Protestant religion, who had flourished under Edward VI, found themselves persecuted.

Elizabeth I sought to establish a middle way, accommodating both parties, but there were still fervent calls for English religion to be 'purified' of traces of Roman Catholic worship. The campaigners for this purge were known as 'Puritans'. The Pilgrim Fathers were essentially committed advocates of the Puritan cause. Unable to secure the reforms they desired, under Elizabeth and subsequently under James I, they took refuge initially in the Netherlands. Then, in 1620, they made the momentous journey to the New World, which seemed to promise an opportunity to create a society regulated according to their own conception of religious truth, without fear of persecution.

Increasingly, with time, emphasis came to fall upon possibilities for material advancement offered by the New World, but to begin with New England was conceived as a place of spiritual renewal. The intense gravity of Nathaniel Hawthorne's Bostonians reflects their awareness of this immense seriousness of Puritan aspirations. Note that back in England, the Civil War, which resulted in the beheading of Charles I, was another momentous attempt to establish a model society run according to Puritan principles. Those events in the Old World were exactly contemporary with the action of *The Scarlet Letter*.

NEW ENGLAND PURITANISM

In 1846, Nathaniel Hawthorne published a collection of stories entitled *Mosses from an Old Manse*. In an essay responding enthusiastically to that volume, Herman Melville noted Nathaniel Hawthorne's 'great power of blackness', and attributed that grave quality to his 'Calvinistic sense of Innate Depravity and Original Sin'. Melville shared that sombre vision, and arguably intensified its effects in Nathaniel Hawthorne. But we can see from 'The Custom-House' that Nathaniel Hawthorne was profoundly conscious of his family's prominence in the history of New England Puritanism, which had John Calvin's teachings as its theological basis.

As he makes clear, *The Scarlet Letter* is set during 'a period when the forms of authority were felt to possess the sacredness of divine institutions' (pp. 59–60). The society in which Hester Prynne lived was theocratic; that is, it was governed according to the unequivocal authority of God's law.

Many of the emigrants from England were fleeing religious persecution, but Nathaniel Hawthorne makes intolerance their own dominant characteristic. Perhaps he was prompted to heighten that aspect through his awareness of later episodes, such as the notorious Salem witch-trials of 1692, in which one of his ancestors was thoroughly implicated.

The Puritan ethos disdained earthly pleasures, and frowned upon physical indulgence of any kind. Music and theatrical entertainments were considered trivial distractions from piety. Food was kept simple, and was eaten in moderation. Puritan dress was uniformly sombre, functional and guaranteed to grant no delight to the eye. Decoration was equated to vanity, so Hester Prynne's elaborate embroidery should be seen as a radical challenge to attitudes underpinning an entire way of life. Note, however, that Nathaniel Hawthorne does refer on a number of occasions to vestiges of a more indulgent taste, in the appearance of Governor Bellingham's house, for example, or in his liking for ale, which some members of the community have preserved, despite their better intentions.

During composition of his novel, Nathaniel Hawthorne consulted Caleb Snow's *A History of Boston* (1825), and Joseph Felt's *The Annals of Salem* (1827), in order to incorporate historically verifiable material. It is

important to recognise, however, that Nathaniel Hawthorne was not
engaged in a systematic factual reconstruction. Dates and details allowed
contemporary readers a sense of the changes which had occurred in New
England over the preceding two centuries, but concern for accuracy was
far less important to Nathaniel Hawthorne than the integrity of his
literary design.

THE DECLARATION OF INDEPENDENCE

It is necessary to remember that when *The Scarlet Letter* was first
published, in 1850, America, as a modern democratic republic, was less
that seventy-five years old. Although political independence from the
Old World had been declared in 1776, the new nation remained heavily
indebted to Europe in cultural terms.

There was concern, felt strongly in Nathaniel Hawthorne's
social circle, that in the mid-nineteenth century the ideals upon which
the new nation had been founded (notably the right to life, liberty and the
pursuit of happiness) were being betrayed, by industrialisation and the
growth of cities, by racial oppression and prejudice, by the unjust
treatment of women, and by engagement in a series of wars. During the
decade preceding publication of *The Scarlet Letter*, movements agitating
for reform, and experimental communities flourished, indicating the
extent to which failure of American aspirations was recognised. Little
more than a decade after Nathaniel Hawthorne's romance appeared,
America was plunged into a disastrous and traumatic Civil War which
had a devastating effect upon the republic's early faith in its glorious
future.

NINETEENTH-CENTURY AMERICAN FEMINISM

In 1848, two years before Nathaniel Hawthorne published *The
Scarlet Letter*, a convention assembled in Seneca Falls, New York,
to establish the basis for political activism in pursuit of women's
rights. The advancement of women was becoming a public issue, as
well as a concern amongst women in Nathaniel Hawthorne's own circle,
including Margaret Fuller and his sister-in-law, Elizabeth Palmer
Peabody.

Nathaniel Hawthorne was highly critical of Fuller's views, and disapproved of the way she conducted her life. Her radical feminist beliefs ignored what he felt were ineradicable and necessary differences between men and women. So when, at the end of *The Scarlet Letter*, Hester expresses a vision which reflects Fuller's own, it is necessary to recognise that Nathaniel Hawthorne draws back from espousing such dissident opinions.

Elizabeth Palmer Peabody was just as insistent as Fuller that the restraints framing women's social activity were artificial, and could readily be cast off. She was the author of twenty-seven books in the fields of theology, sociology and history. The education of women was a special concern for her. Nathaniel Hawthorne, however, withheld his daughters from formal schooling, believing that to be the privilege of males.

LITERARY BACKGROUND

J. HECTOR ST JOHN DE CRÈVECOEUR

In 1782, this immigrant from Normandy published *Letters from an American Farmer*. Six years after the Declaration of Independence it asks the pertinent question, 'What is an American?'. His answer focuses upon self-reliance and freedom from the tyranny of inherited institutions. He also portrays Americans as plants, who have been transplanted from an arid soil in the Old World to a fertile one in the New. Nathaniel Hawthorne clearly cherished a similar faith in the possibilities offered by the new democratic system of government, but in *The Scarlet Letter* he insistently uses the **metaphor** of plants with **irony**. His understanding was that human beings exist in social groups, not in unregulated nature.

THE EMERGENCE OF THE AMERICAN NOVEL

At the time Nathaniel Hawthorne began to write, the taste of American readers was dominated by European, and especially British authors, whose books they found widely available in inexpensive editions. During the Early 1840s, the absence of a working copyright agreement meant that English novelists, such as Charles Dickens and Benjamin Disraeli, received no royalty payments for copies sold in America. However, American writers, such as James Fenimore Cooper had to be paid royalties. In consequence, the imported works were notably cheaper, and that added to the enthusiasm with which they were received.

There was a determination amongst American intellectuals, however, to foster a national literature. It was felt that the arts were an index of cultural health, which had been neglected amidst the basic challenges and the practical difficulties involved in establishing a new society. Cooper (1789–1851), now remembered especially for *The Last of the Mohicans* (1826), set an important example, although his work was characterised by a certain gentility, which reflected his privileged background. Washington Irving (1783–1859) also achieved eminence, but although he is well-known for his story of Rip Van Winkle in the Catskill Mountains, his writing generally is pervaded by the legacy of Old World literary styles and concerns. Edgar Allan Poe (1809–49), recognised today as an extremely significant figure, was viewed by his contemporaries as a curious eccentric, whose obsessions could not be considered representative of America. So, Nathaniel Hawthorne's prose, and the poetry of Walt Whitman (1819–92) were celebrated as the emergence of a distinctive voice, and the foundations for a national literature.

New England Transcendentalism

During the 1830s, a group known as the Transcendentalists became an influential intellectual presence in Boston. The key figure was Ralph Waldo Emerson, arguably the most influential of all American philosophers, and an essayist and poet of considerable talent.

Prominent amongst his followers was Henry David Thoreau, whose *Walden: or Life in the Woods* (1854) remains one of the most singular and compelling works of American literature. Margaret Fuller was another important member of the group, editor of their magazine, *The Dial*, and author of *Woman in the Nineteenth Century* (1845).

Emerson preached that human beings were perfectible, that each individual contains a spark of the divine, and that by breaking down the constraints of received attitudes and inherited conventions of behaviour, a perfect society could be realised on earth. This conception of human nature was the grounding for his faith in democracy, with the basis of political equality being nothing less than the common divinity of men and women. In part the Transcendentalists were responding to perceived injustices and inequalities in American life, and were seeking to regain the promise of an ideal world which the New World had once seemed to offer.

Nathaniel Hawthorne was caught up in the initial excitement, especially as Elizabeth Peabody, sister of his wife Sophia, co-founded *The Dial* with Fuller. In 1841, he entered Brook Farm, an experiment in communal living. At the end of eight months, he declared himself weary of paradise. His disillusionment with Transcendentalist optimism is registered in *The Blithedale Romance* (1852). Margaret Fuller seems to have provided the model for the character, Zenobia.

Nathaniel Hawthorne, who always had reservations, became profoundly sceptical about the Transcendentalist project, with its unbounded aspirations, and anarchistic politics. He shared its concern for the future of American democracy, but increasingly he regarded Transcendentalist idealism as self-deluding, and felt that a surer way for Americans to proceed would follow from acknowledgement of the past, and recognition of the innate sinfulness which, after the Fall from Eden, is the common inheritance of humankind. This view was intensified through his close friendship with the great, and hugely sceptical writer Herman Melville.

The best convenient survey of American literature, including the period in which Nathaniel Hawthorne wrote, remains Marcus Cunliffe's *The Literature of the United States*, fourth edition (Harmondsworth, Penguin, 1986). The classic study of the flowering of American creativity during the mid nineteenth century is F.O. Matthiessen's *American Renaissance* (New York, OUP, 1941).

PART SIX

CRITICAL HISTORY AND BROADER PERSPECTIVES

RECEPTION AND EARLY CRITICAL VIEWS

The Scarlet Letter was received with considerable enthusiasm by American reviewers. Immediately after publication it was declared 'a wonderful book' and 'a tale of thrilling interest' by the *Salem Gazette*. The *Literary World* review noted the book's 'extraordinary power', while the *Boston Daily Times* called it 'the most thoroughly original work of the day'. In England, the *Athenaeum* called it 'a most powerful but painful story', with a 'touch of the fantastic'.

A number of reviewers saw it as evidence that Nathaniel Hawthorne was a writer possessed of genius. In truth, in 1850, any serious attempt by an American to rival the productions of established British authors, such as Walter Scott and Charles Dickens, could be guaranteed a supportive response at home. There were, however, disgruntled voices. Some complained of the immorality of a fiction concerned with an adulterous couple. Others objected to comments in 'The Custom-House', which were taken as bitter personal attacks on Nathaniel Hawthorne's political enemies. He remarked wrily upon these objections in his 'Preface' to the second edition. Such carping was germane to the immediate reception of the book, but in the long-term it seems inconsequential, especially as *The Scarlet Letter* has been constantly in print since its initial publication. Thirty-five pages of reviews by Nathaniel Hawthorne's contemporaries, written following publication of *The Scarlet Letter*, have conveniently been collected in *Nathaniel Hawthorne: The Contemporary Reviews*, edited by John L. Idol, Jr. and Buford Jones (Cambridge, CUP, 1994).

CRITICAL HISTORY

In 1879, Henry James, who later became one the most eminent American novelists, published a study entitled *Hawthorne* (London, Macmillan, 1967 – edited by Tony Tanner). It surveys the life and work of his predecessor, and locates him within nineteenth-century American culture. James remarks that when *The Scarlet Letter* first appeared, in 1850, it was the finest work of imaginative literature to have been produced in the United States. He also notes its critical reception, which generally took pride in the fact that an American had written a work of literature to bear favourable comparison with the literature of Europe. It did so, moreover, without compromising its distinctive American character.

James admired the romance, but he did have certain reservations, especially concerning the symbolism, which he felt was overdone. In particular, he disliked the scarlet 'A' glowing in the sky above Dimmesdale's midnight vigil. He felt that the scene verges on comedy, or as he put it, 'is in danger of crossing the line that separates the sublime from its intimate neighbour'.

In 1923, the English novelist D.H. Lawrence devoted two chapters to Nathaniel Hawthorne in his book, *Studies in Classic American Literature* (Harmondsworth, Penguin, 1971). The second addresses *The Blithedale Romance*; the first is essentially concerned with *The Scarlet Letter*. Lawrence's assessment is characteristically idiosyncratic, but is packed with suggestive insights. He argues, for example, that Dimmesdale and Chillingworth represent two halves of 'manhood', engaged in mutual destruction, and he is bold enough to link the 'A' with both Adam and America itself.

An important development in the history of the book's reception occurred in 1953, with publication of Charles Feidelson's *Symbolism and American Literature* (Chicago, Chicago UP, 1953). Feidelson pointed out that *The Scarlet Letter*, while obviously indebted to the allegorical examples of Spenser and Bunyan, could not be classed as simply an allegory. In its openness to multiple meanings, the book was more properly a symbolist work, and as such, Feidelson argued, it helped inaugurate the technical innovations of modern literature.

Critical evaluation has remained high, and 1964 saw the scholarly production of a Centenary Edition of the complete works, by the Ohio State University Center for Textual Studies. Roy Harvey Pearce edited *Hawthorne Centenary Essays* (Columbus, Ohio State UP, 1964). Subsequent noteworthy collections include *Nathaniel Hawthorne: New Critical Essays*, edited by A. Robert Lee (London, Vision Press, 1982), and *Modern Critical Views*, edited by Harold Bloom (New York, Chelsea House, 1986). A brief, but instructive survey of critical trends is provided in Michael J. Colacurcio's editorial introduction to another illuminating volume, *New Essays on The Scarlet Letter* (Cambridge, CUP, 1985).

CONTEMPORARY APPROACHES

PSYCHOANALYTIC

Psychoanalytic criticism reads literary works in relation to theories of the dynamic unconscious, initially formulated by Sigmund Freud (1856–1939). Freud argued that impulses which threaten the coherence of our sense of self, and the orderliness of our social organisation, are 'repressed'. That is, they are consigned to the unconscious part of our nature. The conscious mind has no direct access to this murky region, but Freud stressed that the potentially destructive impulses which are stored there must find an outlet in some form.

Dreams are a primary means for the unconscious to unburden itself. Freud saw them as a kind of **symbolic** language, translating what has been repressed into a form that lends itself to interpretation. He also claimed that the unconscious determines our behaviour in all sorts of ways of which we are not consciously aware. These includes slips of the tongue, and misplacing or losing objects. For Freud, the unconscious played a dynamic role in our everyday lives, motivating our actions.

If repressed urges do not find adequate release they are manifested as symptoms of what we generally recognise as mental illness. In reading *The Scarlet Letter*, we can see Arthur Dimmesdale as a suitable case-study for Freudian psychoanalysis. He has broken the rules that govern his community. If he were to admit publicly that he had succumbed to sexual temptation, his sense of self (in Freud's terms, his 'ego') would collapse, and the stability of Boston society would experience temporary disruption. So, the transgression is repressed, consigned to the dark regions of his being.

It must find its outlet, however, and it does so, in part, through the placing of his hand upon his breast, over his heart. Pearl regularly passes comment upon this recurrent action. Freud also would have taken note of this symptom of mental disturbance, or obsessional neurosis. More dramatically, the minister's carving of a scarlet 'A' in his own flesh is a graphic demonstration of the Freudian principle that the repressed must find expression, in some form.

Note that in Freud's theory, potentially dangerous impulses are often sexual in character. The contract of marriage can be seen to provide a social framework for rendering human sexual impulses legitimate. Hester Prynne and Dimmesdale have been lovers outside of that framework, and have in fact violated the existing contract between Hester and Chillingworth. In Freudian terminology, the community acts as an external representation of the 'super-ego', that component of the self which should exercise a restraining and moralising function. Freud felt that it is through such regulation that 'civilisation' survives the constant threat lurking in the animalistic, or instinctive aspects of human behaviour, which he called the 'id'.

A psychoanalytic reading would recognise the stylised landscape of this romance as conforming to the compartmentalised Freudian model of human nature. A space such as the market-place might be seen to correspond to the public self (or 'ego'). The forest corresponds to unruly instinct (or 'id'). The prison and the scaffold correspond to the monitoring conscience (or 'super-ego').

Nathaniel Hawthorne's work, with its introspection, its concern for a present bearing the inheritance of past actions, and its burden of guilt, lends itself readily to Freudian analysis, although the practice sits uncomfortably close to Nathaniel Hawthorne's conception of the 'Unpardonable Sin', violation of the sanctity of another person's soul. As well as applying the analytical method to literary texts, Freudian criticism has set to work on authors themselves, seeking to uncover the unconscious motivation for the writer's choice of themes and style of writing. *The Scarlet Letter* was published six years before Freud's birth, but in 'The Custom-House' Nathaniel Hawthorne anticipates psychoanalytic reading with his suggestion that the romance that follows is a means to come to terms with the guilt he feels on account of William Hathorne's brutal behaviour. Freud saw art as a means granting an outlet to repression, without jeopardising the integrity of self and society. Such 'sublimation', as he called it, might be reflected in Hester's needlecraft.

A classic example of the psychoanalytic approach is Frederick Crews, *The Sins of the Fathers: Hawthorne's Psychological Themes* (Oxford, OUP, 1966). Chapter VIII, 'The Ruined Wall', is specifically concerned with *The Scarlet Letter*, while the concluding chapter considers 'Hawthorne, Freud, and Literary Value'.

Feminist

The term 'feminist criticism' refers to a range of approaches crucially concerned with the representation of women, their personal identities, and their social relationships within a society dominated by men. The fate of Hester Prynne obviously makes *The Scarlet Letter* a work of considerable interest to critics favouring a feminist approach.

The crucial issue is whether Nathaniel Hawthorne has portrayed Hester as an admirable figure, who has transcended the limits placed upon women and their experience in the mid-nineteenth century, or whether she is ultimately to be seen as a sinful transgressor, who has deserved to be made an outcast. Some feminist critics might use this issue in order to gauge Nathaniel Hawthorne's response to contemporary agitation for the social advancement of women. Others might take *The Scarlet Letter* as a focal point for analysis of the more general cultural impact of that agitation.

Feminist criticism must initially welcome Nathaniel Hawthorne's unsympathetic portrayal of the Puritan patriarchy of seventeenth-century Boston. But it is likely to see his liberal embrace of softening attitudes as a strategy to preserve the *status quo*. In other words, Nathaniel Hawthorne clearly disapproved of the sternness and inflexibility of New England Puritanism, but feminist analysis might disclose that he approved of amelioration only to the extent that it left relationships between men and women essentially unchanged, with the dominant male role unchallenged.

Similarly, although *The Scarlet Letter* is evidently a book which aims to counter simplistic interpretation by disclosing complex realities lurking behind compact symbols and images, feminist criticism might investigate ways in which Nathaniel Hawthorne's characterisation of Hester is actually promoting stereotypes. It is possible to argue that he has cast Hester as a temptress, a latterday Eve luring a modern Adam to his downfall. Such characterisation seems to close down rather than open up interpretative possibilities. Hester is alternatively presented as an angel of mercy, attending the sick and needy. This equally endorses a well-established stereotype of specifically female aptitudes and inclinations; it is an extension of the lot assigned to wife and mother, containing woman's essential role narrowly within the domestic sphere.

It might be argued that by showing Hester to be an exemplary artist, Nathaniel Hawthorne is actually elevating her above household routine, and is drawing a parallel with his own activity as a writer. Certainly, *The Scarlet Letter* insists upon the necessity for art within human society, as a vital means to ensure balance between head and heart. But biographical information indicates that Nathaniel Hawthorne disapproved of women writers. He regarded embroidery as unequivocally a lesser art, while acknowledging that it had long been the principal means for female expression. In an important reassessment of needlecraft, the feminist historian Rozsika Parker has argued that 'to know the history of embroidery is to know the history of women'. Although there is no direct mention of Nathaniel Hawthorne in her book, *The Subversive Stitch: Embroidery and the Making of the Feminine* (London, Routledge, 1989), it is a study which illuminates the significance of Hester Prynne's skill as a seamstress.

A brief, yet helpful survey of twentieth-century feminist criticism can be found in Louise A. DeSalvo's *Nathaniel Hawthorne* (Brighton, Harvester Press, 1987). The book also offers an overview of developments in nineteenth-century feminism, before engaging critically with *The Scarlet Letter*, and Nathaniel Hawthorne's other American romances. DeSalvo finds Nathaniel Hawthorne guilty of offering, in *The Scarlet Letter*, a distorted version of the past, which plays down the cruelty of Puritan punishment, and effectively exculpates his intolerant and persecutory ancestors.

Gloria C. Erlich's *Family Themes and Hawthorne's Fiction: The Tenacious Web* (New Brunswick, N.J., Rutgers, 1984), is another noteworthy example of a feminist approach. Erlich explores Nathaniel Hawthorne's portrayal of women in relation to the impact upon him made by significant circumstances of his own life, especially his relationships with his mother and his sister.

SEMIOTIC

Semiotics, or semiology, is the study of literary texts and of social practices viewed as structures composed from signs. It has its basis in the linguistic theories of Ferdinand de Saussure, and has been refined by later critics such as Roland Barthes and Umberto Eco.

For the semiotician, human cultures are formed from 'codes', or systems of meaning. 'Signs' are the components of these codes. Jonathan Culler, in *Framing the Sign* (Oxford, Blackwell, 1988), has suggested that semiotics can most readily be understood by consideration through consideration of the habitual behaviour of tourists. So, for example, visitors to London may 'read' the red buses, the distinctive uniforms worn by policemen, and landmarks, such as the tower containing the bell known as Big Ben, as signs disclosing the 'Londonness' of London. If those buses were yellow or blue they would belong to another code, and would not tell the tourist that he or she were in the capital city of England. Similarly, if the police wore baseball caps, rather than their distinctively shaped helmets, tourists would not be able to read 'Londonness' with the same immediacy and confidence.

In *The Scarlet Letter* we are invited to visit seventeenth-century Boston, with the narrator as our tour-guide. He also is travelling back in time, and he points out to us ways in which the codes forming 'New England' have altered during the intervening years. From the start of his narrative, he is identifying signs that comprise the system of New World Puritanism. The 'sad-colored garments and gray, steeple-crowned hats' (p. 45) form part of the Puritan dress-code. The richly embroidered garments worn by Pearl show that she does not belong to the culture of Puritanism.

This distinction reveals that reading signs is not just a matter of recognising the context you are in; it crucially discloses views upon reality, and systems of belief. The horizons of Puritan understanding are to be read from the appearance of the Bostonians. Pearl's appearance locates her beyond those horizons. The political and ethical disclosures to be made through semiotic analysis were pursued vigorously by the French critic Roland Barthes. He was particularly concerned with ways in which we come to take for granted systems of signs which have been assembled for a particular purpose. We come to regard as natural, codes which in fact have a history. So, for example, we might visit a large house and see it as a sign of affluence and good taste. We may not pause, however, to consider the labour involved in construction of the building, and the relationships involving power that have existed between the labourers and the subsequent occupants. Barthes used the term 'mythologies' to identify our habit of concealing sensitive political and ethical issues behind our tendency to take for granted, and to accept as 'natural' the existence of an environment, or a set of social practices.

With the scarlet 'A' at its heart, Nathaniel Hawthorne's text is inescapably concerned with the processes of signification, and *The Scarlet Letter* can be seen as a treatise of semiology, written half a century before Saussure formally conceived the practice. Indeed, Nathaniel Hawthorne's reference to the warlike American eagle carved above the Salem Custom House exposes an aggressive, imperial 'mythology' within the institutions of the Republic, in a manner which can be seen to anticipate Barthes.

A helpful introduction to this approach is Terence Hawkes, *Structuralism and Semiotics* (London, Routledge – New Accents, 1977). For a specific discussion of Nathaniel Hawthorne, see Millicent Bell's essay, 'The Obliquity of Signs: *The Scarlet Letter*', in *The Massachusetts Review* 23 (1982).

World events	Hawthorne's life	Literary events
		1590 Edmund Spenser, *The Faerie Queen*
1603 James I accedes to throne		
1605 Guy Fawkes arrested and conspiracy to kill James I is discovered		
1606 William Brewster leads a group of Separatists to Leiden to escape religious persecution in England		
1607 First real English settlement in North America at Jamestown, Virginia		
1618-48 Thirty Years' War		
1620 102 men, women and children leave Plymouth for America; Pilgrim Fathers arrive at Plymouth Rock		
1625 Charles I accedes to throne		
1629 Massachusetts Bay Company granted charter and colony of Massachusetts is formed		
	1630 Major William Hathorne arrives in Massachusetts	
1642-6 First English Civil War		
1648 Second English Civil War		
1649 Charles I executed; England is declared a commonwealth		
		1651 Thomas Hobbes, *Leviathan*
1658 Cromwell dies		
1660 Charles II accedes to throne		
		1667 John Milton, *Paradise Lost*
		1678 John Bunyan, *The Pilgrim's Progress*
1685 James II accedes; Dominion of New England formed		
		1687 Isaac Newton, *Principia*
1689 William and Mary of Orange become sovereigns of England		
		1690 John Locke, *An Essay Concerning Human Understanding*

World events	Hawthorne's life	Literary events
1691 New Royal Charter granted to the colony of Massachusetts – ending control of the Massachusetts government by Puritan religious leaders		
1692 Salem witchcraft trials		
		1726 Jonathan Swift, *Gulliver's Travels*
		1748 David Hume, *An Enquiry Concerning Human Understanding*
1760 French forces defeated in North America		
1763 End of Seven Years' War		
		1766 Oliver Goldsmith, *The Vicar of Wakefield*
1775-83 American Revolution		
1776 Thomas Jefferson writes The Declaration of Independence		
		1782 St John de Crèvecoeur, *Letters from an American Farmer*
1783 Independence of American colonies is recognised		
1787 Constitution of United States is written		
1788 George Washington is elected as first US President		
		1789 William Blake, *Songs of Innocence*
		1791 Mary Wollstonecraft, *A Vindication of the Rights of Women*
		1798 Samuel Taylor Coleridge (with William Wordsworth), *Lyrical Ballads*
	1804 Nathaniel Hawthorne born 4th July	
1805 Louisiana purchase		
	1808 His father dies	
		1809 Washington Irving, *A History of New York*

World events	Hawthorne's life	Literary events
		1810 Walter Scott, *The Lady of the Lake*
1812-15 War between Great Britain and US		
		1813 Jane Austen, *Pride and Prejudice*
		1817 Samuel Taylor Coleridge, *Biographia Literaria*
		1820 Percy Bysshe Shelley, *Prometheus Unbound*
	1821 Becomes a student at Bowdoin College	
1823 Monroe Doctrine		
	1825 Graduates and returns to Salem	**1825** Caleb Snow, *A History of Boston*
		1826 James Fenimore Cooper, *The Last of the Mohicans;* Benjamin Disraeli, *Vivien Grey*
		1827 Joseph Felt, *The Annals of Salem;* James Fenimore Cooper, *The Prairie*
	1828 *Fanshawe*	
	1836 Moves to Boston and works as a magazine editor	
1837 Queen Victoria accedes to the British throne	**1837** *Twice-Told Tales*	
	1839 Works at Boston Custom House	
		1840 Ralph Waldo Emerson and Margaret Fuller found *The Dial*
	1841 Resigns from the Boston Custom House and returns to Salem; joins Brook Farm Communitarian experiment (for 8 weeks); *Grandfather's Chair; A History for Youth*	**1841** Ralph Waldo Emerson, *Essays* (first series)
	1842 Marries Sophia Peabody	**1842** Ralph Waldo Emerson, *Essays* (second series)

World events	Hawthorne's life	Literary events
	1843 'The Birthmark'; 'The Celestial Railroad'	**1843** Edgar Allan Poe, 'The Gold Bug'
	1844 Una is born	
		1845 Margaret Fuller, *Women in the Nineteenth Century*
	1846 Julian born; appointed Surveyor at Salem Custom House; *Mosses from an Old Manse*	
		1847 Emily Brontë, *Wuthering Heights*
1848 US wins Mexican War; first Women's Rights Convention		
	1849 Leaves Salem Custom House	
	1850 Meets Herman Melville; *The Scarlet Letter*	
	1851 Rosa born; 'Ethan Brand'; *The House of Seven Gables*	**1851** Herman Melville, *Moby-Dick*
	1852 *The Blithedale Romance; A Wonder Book for Girls and Boys; The Snow Image and Other Twice-Told Tales*	**1852** Harriet Beecher Stowe, *Uncle Tom's Cabin*
	1853 Travels to England as an American Consul	
		1854 Henry David Thoreau, *Walden: or Life in the Woods*
		1855 Walt Whitman, *Leaves of Grass* (1st edition)
	1858 Travels to France and Italy	
	1860 Returns to US; *The Marble Faun*	**1860** George Eliot, *The Mill on the Floss*
1861 Southern slave states secede from American Union and form the Confederate States; American Civil War		**1861** Charles Dickens, *Great Expectations*
	1863 *Our Old Home*	
	1864 Dies	
		1865 Walt Whitman, *Drum-Taps*

World events	Hawthorne's life	Literary events
1865 End of American Civil War; Slavery is abolished in US; President Abraham Lincoln is assassinated		
1867 The US purchases Alaska from the Russians		
	1868 *American Notebooks*	
1870-90 The last Native American tribes are defeated by government forces and confined to reservations	**1870** *English Notebooks*	
	1871 *French and Italian Notebooks*	
	1872 *Septimus Felton*	
	1876 *The Dolliver Romance*	**1876** Mark Twain, *Tom Sawyer*
		1877 Bronson Alcott, *Table Talk*
		1879 Henry James, *Hawthorne*
		1881 Henry James, *Portrait of a Lady*
	1883 *Dr Grimshawe's Secret; The Ancestral Footsteps*	
		1884 Mark Twain, *Huckleberry Finn*
		1891 Thomas Hardy, *Tess of the D'Urbervilles*
		1903 George Bernard Shaw, *Man and Superman*
		1911 Edith Wharton, *Ethan Frome*
		1913 D.H. Lawrence, *Sons and Lovers*
1914-18 First World War		
		1922 James Joyce, *Ulysses*
		1924 E.M. Forster, *A Passage to India*
		1925 F. Scott Fitzgerald, *The Great Gatsby.* Theodore Dreiser, *An American Tragedy*
		1929 Ernest Hemingway, *A Farewell to Arms*

allegory a narrative which has a coherent structure of meaning beyond its apparent, surface meaning

ambivalence the unresolved co-existence of seemingly opposed, even mutually exclusive meanings, or the openness of a text to divergent interpretations

caricature grotesque rendering of character through exaggeration of personality traits

conceits literary formulations which are characterised by bold comparisons or connections, drawn between apparently dissimilar or remote objects or concepts

defamiliarisation the capacity of some kinds of writing to strip away familiarity from the world about us, so that we see things anew

Gothic fictional mode concentrating on the bizarre, macabre, or aberrant psychological states

irony saying one thing while meaning another

melodrama writing which relies upon sensational happenings, violent action, and improbable events

metaphor description of one thing as being another thing

Metaphysicals term applied to a group of seventeenth-century poets, including John Donne, George Herbert and Andrew Marvell. The group was characterised by a taste for witty play with ideas, often pushing logic to its limits

metonymy substitution of the name of a thing by the name of an attribute of it, or something closely associated with it

parable a short narrative devised to give a clear demonstration of a moral or lesson

pastoral literary mode contrasting the virtue of a simple life with the corruption of sophistication and complexity

persona an assumed guise, adopted deliberately by an author or narrator

personification the attribution of human qualities to an idea or concept

polysemy the capacity of signs, including words, to have multiple meanings

psychological realism a mode of fiction which renders the inner lives of characters, rather than concentrating on external actions

romance in Nathaniel Hawthorne's terms, a narrative that blends the Actual and the Imaginary

Romantic referring to a phase in English literature between 1789 and 1830, characterised by a heightened emphasis upon human feelings and the vital force of nature

satire writing which exposes and ridicules human foibles

semiotics the study of signs, also known as 'semiology'. Although derived from the linguistic work of Ferdinand de Saussure, semiotics extends its field of study to all patterned systems of communications

simile a weak form of metaphor, in which one thing is said to be like another

symbol a sign which represents something else, by analogy or association

Author of this note

Dr Julian Cowley taught English at King's College London before joining the University of Luton, where he is Senior Lecturer in Literary Studies.

NOTES

York Notes Advanced (£3.99 each)

Margaret Atwood
The Handmaid's Tale

Jane Austen
Mansfield Park

Jane Austen
Persuasion

Jane Austen
Pride and Prejudice

Alan Bennett
Talking Heads

William Blake
*Songs of Innocence and of
Experience*

Charlotte Brontë
Jane Eyre

Emily Brontë
Wuthering Heights

Geoffrey Chaucer
The Franklin's Tale

Geoffrey Chaucer
*General Prologue to the
Canterbury Tales*

Geoffrey Chaucer
*The Wife of Bath's Prologue
and Tale*

Joseph Conrad
Heart of Darkness

Charles Dickens
Great Expectations

John Donne
Selected Poems

George Eliot
The Mill on the Floss

F. Scott Fitzgerald
The Great Gatsby

E.M. Forster
A Passage to India

Brian Friel
Translations

Thomas Hardy
The Mayor of Casterbridge

Thomas Hardy
Tess of the d'Urbervilles

Seamus Heaney
*Selected Poems from Opened
Ground*

Nathaniel Hawthorne
The Scarlet Letter

James Joyce
Dubliners

John Keats
Selected Poems

Christopher Marlowe
Doctor Faustus

Arthur Miller
Death of a Salesman

Toni Morrison
Beloved

William Shakespeare
Antony and Cleopatra

William Shakespeare
As You Like It

William Shakespeare
Hamlet

William Shakespeare
King Lear

William Shakespeare
Measure for Measure

William Shakespeare
The Merchant of Venice

William Shakespeare
Much Ado About Nothing

William Shakespeare
Othello

William Shakespeare
Romeo and Juliet

William Shakespeare
The Tempest

William Shakespeare
The Winter's Tale

Mary Shelley
Frankenstein

Alice Walker
The Color Purple

Oscar Wilde
*The Importance of Being
Earnest*

Tennessee Williams
A Streetcar Named Desire

John Webster
The Duchess of Malfi

W.B. Yeats
Selected Poems

GCSE and equivalent levels (£3.50 each)

Maya Angelou
I Know Why the Caged Bird Sings

Jane Austen
Pride and Prejudice

Alan Ayckbourn
Absent Friends

Elizabeth Barrett Browning
Selected Poems

Robert Bolt
A Man for All Seasons

Harold Brighouse
Hobson's Choice

Charlotte Brontë
Jane Eyre

Emily Brontë
Wuthering Heights

Shelagh Delaney
A Taste of Honey

Charles Dickens
David Copperfield

Charles Dickens
Great Expectations

Charles Dickens
Hard Times

Charles Dickens
Oliver Twist

Roddy Doyle
Paddy Clarke Ha Ha Ha

George Eliot
Silas Marner

George Eliot
The Mill on the Floss

William Golding
Lord of the Flies

Oliver Goldsmith
She Stoops To Conquer

Willis Hall
The Long and the Short and the Tall

Thomas Hardy
Far from the Madding Crowd

Thomas Hardy
The Mayor of Casterbridge

Thomas Hardy
Tess of the d'Urbervilles

Thomas Hardy
The Withered Arm and other Wessex Tales

L.P. Hartley
The Go-Between

Seamus Heaney
Selected Poems

Susan Hill
I'm the King of the Castle

Barry Hines
A Kestrel for a Knave

Louise Lawrence
Children of the Dust

Harper Lee
To Kill a Mockingbird

Laurie Lee
Cider with Rosie

Arthur Miller
The Crucible

Arthur Miller
A View from the Bridge

Robert O'Brien
Z for Zachariah

Frank O'Connor
My Oedipus Complex and other stories

George Orwell
Animal Farm

J.B. Priestley
An Inspector Calls

Willy Russell
Educating Rita

Willy Russell
Our Day Out

J.D. Salinger
The Catcher in the Rye

William Shakespeare
Henry IV Part 1

William Shakespeare
Henry V

William Shakespeare
Julius Caesar

William Shakespeare
Macbeth

William Shakespeare
The Merchant of Venice

William Shakespeare
A Midsummer Night's Dream

William Shakespeare
Much Ado About Nothing

William Shakespeare
Romeo and Juliet

William Shakespeare
The Tempest

William Shakespeare
Twelfth Night

George Bernard Shaw
Pygmalion

Mary Shelley
Frankenstein

R.C. Sherriff
Journey's End

Rukshana Smith
Salt on the snow

John Steinbeck
Of Mice and Men

Robert Louis Stevenson
Dr Jekyll and Mr Hyde

Jonathan Swift
Gulliver's Travels

Robert Swindells
Daz 4 Zoe

Mildred D. Taylor
Roll of Thunder, Hear My Cry

Mark Twain
Huckleberry Finn

James Watson
Talking in Whispers

William Wordsworth
Selected Poems

A Choice of Poets

Mystery Stories of the Nineteenth Century including The Signalman

Nineteenth Century Short Stories

Poetry of the First World War

Six Women Poets